FEBRUARY 1988

Volkswagen designer Ferdinand Porsche in 1944 with Beetle in Prague.

Contents

Preface

At the time of its development in the thirties the technical concept of the Volkswagen was so advanced that it remained one of the best in the world for half a century. Reliability, robustness and versatility were the reasons for its success. Regular revision throughout its entire production kept it constantly ahead of its competitors.

But had it been only for these rational advantages the Volkswagen would perhaps have just remained one car among many. What made it an actual 'people's car' was its acceptance by the customers, which was based on more than a pinch of emotion. For the majority of its owners the Beetle – and the nickname itself is a very personal thing – was not just a bit of technology, a means of transport, but a real member of the family that just happened to live in the garage or under the streetlamp.

And as a member of the family the Beetle was naturally looked after, cared for and cosmetically 'improved'. Vases with real or, for better keeping, artificial flowers gave a cosy atmosphere inside it, additional chrome turned the little car into a 'mobile castle' for personal security among the perils of the road.

It was an ambassador of Germany throughout the world, in all climatic zones and cultural regions. This was reflected in constant increases in production up to its zenith.

Nobody was indifferent to the Beetle. This personal relationship between the Volkswagen and its owner still finds expression today in the many objects based on the Beetle.

This is also a kind of comment on and honouring of this worthy automobile: unique in its history, its technology, its appearance which remained almost unchanged for decades, its astronomical production records, its popularity.

All this made and makes the Beetle a product which is a phenomenon and which we believe will maintain its influence even into the next century.

Dr. C.H. Hahn.

Chairman of the Board
Volkswagen AG

Two early forerunners of the Beetle: The Porsche Types 12 and 32. Ferdinand Porsche built the forefather of the VW Beetle, the Type 12 in 1932 for Zündapp; three prototypes were produced.

The Type 32 was developed in 1934 for NSU. The three NSU prototypes already boast almost all the typical Beetle design features. The only car still in existence can be seen in the Wolfsburg Auto-Museum.

This is how Ferdinand Porsche saw the Volkswagen in his own mind. The drawing is from 1932.

One for all

The story of the VW Beetle

When people talk about the Volkswagen they automatically think of the VW Beetle. Not that the Volkswagen got its entirely appropriate nickname at home in Germany, as one might think, but in its second home, the USA.

Here the Beetle succeeded where many foreign competitors failed: It got accepted. Without reservation. Here this strange beast 'made in Germany' immediately made lots of friends.

In the USA, the land of (almost) endless possiblities, there also sprang up a whole series of in part decidedly bizarre Beetle stylings, 'special bugs', curiosities. We want to show you some of these in our book.

Even today the Beetle is popular with many Americans, and this despite the fact that this veteran has not been imported into the USA as a new car since 1977. The reason for this is the stiffer safety and emission regulations.

In the homeland of the Beetle, the Federal Republic of Germany, the situation is now similar. Over a million Beetles are still driving on Germany's roads. Despite falling registrations – last year only some 10,000 VW enthusiasts decided on the Beetle – it is still one of the most popular and best-loved cars of all.

When on 15th May 1981 in the Volkswagen branch factory at Puebla, Mexico, some 120 kilometres east of the capital Mexico City, the 20-millionth Beetle came off the line, this was an all-time record in the history of the automobile and one which is unlikely ever to be broken.

Even Henry Ford's best-selling Model I, the Tin Lizzie, 'only' managed around fifteen million examples during its production life of just under twenty years.

An early Volkswagen prototype, built in 1935 and designated V1. The similarity to the later mass-production Beetle is startling.

In the Market Square in Tübingen, 1935: Ferry Porsche at the wheel of the experimental vehicle V2.

In the course of a continuous-running test drive in the spring of 1937, the Type VW 30 pre-production prototypes (29 saloons and one convertible), built at the Daimler-Benz body shop in Sindelfingen, covered some 2,4 million test kilometers without a serious fault. The Porsche development had proved itself in brilliant style.

Technically the veteran Beetle, despite all attempts at updating, must be regarded as old-fashioned, and compared with the modern Volkswagen designs completely outdated and no longer competitive.

What remains is the legend of the everlasting Beetle. Only dyed-in-the-wool Beetle enthusiasts, of which there are still quite a few, keep faith with the omnipresent animal.

The reasons for the unparalleled global success of the Beetle can be found simply and solely in its conception, production fifty years ago by Ferdinand Porsche.

Furthermore the Beetle survives owing to its patent qualities: solid workmanship, good equipment and above all its proverbial reliability – it runs and runs and runs .

Additional reasons for the Beetle phenomenon are doubtless its low purchase price and high resale value even after years of use.

And a Beetle is low on maintenance costs, especially for repairs.

Nor was the Beetle ever misused as a status symbol. There is no such thing, according to an analysis of the office of statistics of the US automotive industry, as a typical Beetle driver. They cannot, as a result, be put into any kind of convenient pigeon-hole Rather they come from all kinds of population groups and all kinds of occupation. The Beetle is a classless automobile in a class-conscious society.

This study carried out in the sixties is still perfectly valid. The US magazine LIFE put it like this: 'A VW is a member of the family that just happens to live in the garage'.

Maybe exaggerated, but a nonetheless apt designation of the well-loved Beetle. When over 50 years ago Ferdinand Porsche started on the development work for a people's car he could not of course foresee that he was laying the foundation stone of the most successful and perhaps best-loved automobile of all time.

At the end of the September 1931 Porsche received from the Nuremberg Zündapp works, one of the biggest German motorcycle manufacturers, a commission to develop a low-cost four seat passenger car.

First to emerge were three experimental cars called Porsche Type 12 equipped with water-cooled five-cylinder radial engines at the rear driving the rear wheels. The gearbox was in front of the rear axle and formed a unit with the final drive

One of the three experimental cars of the VW-3 series of 1936. The headlights are still mounted in the nose, the doors are hinged at the central pillars.

Five of 30 Type VW 30 pre-production cars. Although the test drives were carried out in strictest secrecy, contact with the public could not be avoided. Wherever the Volkswagen appeared, heads were turned.

Ferdinand Porsche (2nd from left) and a VW 30. A typical scene, for Porsche lost no opportunity of taking the wheel of his brainchild.

This power train arrangement, tried in practice for the first time in the Type 12, was subsequently to prove itself millions of times over in the VW Beetle. However for reasons of cost Zündapp dropped its people's car project and went on building mo torcycles.

In 1933 NSU, another well-known motorcycle manufacturer, asked Porsche to design a modern economical car for subsequent series production. With this Porsche was at last able to realise his idea of an air-cooled rear engine. As early as the beginning of 1934 the plans were ready for the NSU car, the Porsche Type 32. This already had the design characteristics typical of all later Volkswagens – the central tube platform frame, independent suspension, a torsion spring axle with double suspension arms in front and a swing axle at the rear also with torsion springs, shock absorbers and drum brakes on all four wheels which at that time were by no means a matter of course. Thus the NSU used for the first time torsion springs instead of leaf springs, an idea of Porsche's. The heart of the vehicle however was the air-cooled boxer engine with two pairs of horizontally-opposed cylinders, a belt-driven cooler blower, 1.5 litres swept volume and 20 bhp.

Three vehicles were built and thoroughly tested; nonetheless the NSU small car also failed to go into series production. Instead NSU brought a people's motorcycle on the market, the NSU 'Quickly'.

At the beginning of 1934 Porsche presented to the Reich Ministry of Transport his 'proposal concerning the construction of a German people's car', a study in which Porsche stated his attitude to the concept of 'Volksauto'.

In Porsche's view a people's car should not be a small car but a utility vehicle with normal dimensions but relatively low weight.

After intensive discussion between government offices and the Reich association of the German automotive industry (RDA), on 22nd June 1934 the RDA and Porsche concluded an agreement by which Porsche undertook to deliver the first Volkswagen prototype within only ten months. A further clause in the contract provided that on the basis of a 50,000-unit production run the car should cost no more than 990 Marks. The RDA, which at first viewed Porsche's Volkswagen project with the utmost scepticism, financed it to the tune of 20,000 Marks per month.

It was soon apparent that neither the time set nor

26th May 1938: Laying the cornerstone for the Volkswagen works near Fallersleben, today a district of Wolfsburg.

Roofing ceremony at the Volkswagen works in April 1939.

After the laying of the cornerstone, these three Volkswagens of the pre-production series VW 38 (saloon, roller roof saloon and convertible) were officially revealed. Instead of Volkswagen the Beetle was now to be called 'KdF-Wagen' (KdF = Kraft durch Freude – Strength through Joy).

the financing was by any means sufficient. In spite of this, at the cost of great effort the first five Volkswagen prototypes of Porsche design appeared between 1934 and 1936: the V1, V2 and the VW3 series.

To begin with various engines were experimented with including a two-cylinder four-stroke and a two-cylinder double-piston two-stroke; in the end the four-cylinder four-stroke familiar from the NSU was decided upon. But these first boxer engines did not prove 'motorwayproof' in practice. This problem too was solved after comprehensive modifications.

Under the constant supervision of the RDA the prototypes of the VW3 series began a 50,000 kilometre endurance test drive on 10th October 1936. The three vehicles bore up astoundingly well. Despite initial scepticism the Porsche design proved itself splendidly. In the final report of the RDA the verdict was: 'The vehicle showed qualities which appear to recommend themselves for further development'

Now Hitler in person pressed for the Volkswagen project – from which he anticipated a great propaganda effect – to be gone with full steam ahead. The motor manufacturers belonging to the RDA however did not see themselves in a position to further develop the Volkswagen to series production level under the conditions set without State subsidy and then sell it at the fixed price of only 990 Marks.

Porsche had meanwhile conceived a replacement design, a pre-series car of which 30 were built at the Daimler Benz bodywork factory in Sindelfingen and at Reutter's in Stuttgart. On account of this the cars had the designation VW 30 and already bore a strong similarity to the subsequent Beetle.

The VW 30 project was carried out in the strictest secrecy, veiled from the public which although it had heard a great deal of the Volkswagen had never seen one. All told the 30 pre-series Volkswagens covered nearly 2.5 million test kilometres without serious breakdowns, thus finally proving that Porsche's concept was the right one.

Finally in 1938 the entire Volkswagen project was taken over by the National Socialist leisure organisation 'Strength Through Joy' (KdF). Financed by the KdF a further 44 pre-series vehicles were produced at Reutter's in Stuttgart. With this model, known as VW 38, the Volkswagen was given its final shape. A further series, the VW 39, was not

Kalkulation des Volkswagens.

Das Jahr der Proklamation des KdF Wagens	19
	37
Grundsteinlegung zum KdF-Wagenwerk	26.
	5.
	19
	38
Geschwindigkeit in km/st.	100
Anzahl der PS	24
Benzinverbrauch in ltr/100 km	7
Länge d. Wagens in cm	420
Breite " " "	150
Höhe " " "	145
Errechneter Preis	RM 990

The Volkswagen was to cost only 990 Marks; that was roughly the price of a small motorcycle with 350 c.c. engine displacement.

1938 KdF models: Above the saloon, which had an optional roller roof; below the convertible.

continued. At about the same time KdF employees agreed the final location for the Volkswagen factory in which the Volkswagen was to be built on the American pattern in mass production.

On 26th May 1938, Ascension Day, Hitler laid the foundation stone of the Volkswagen factory on the bank of the Mitteland canal near the small town of Fallersleben. He promised then that 'every working German' should have the opportunity of buying his own KdF car (as the Volkswagen was from then on to be known) for only 990 Marks. An astonishingly low price; it was about the same as that of a 350 cc motorcycle.

On 1st August 1938 a special saving scheme was introduced with the aim of enabling all prospective customers to save up the 990 Marks.

But it was not to be. On 1st September 1939 the second World War broke out. Production planned for the KdF car had to be postponed indefinitely. Armaments had priority. And so the dream of a car of their own never became reality for the 336,668 savers.

Meanwhile at the Volkswagen factory Type 82 military vehicles based on Porsche's Volkswagen and Type 128 and 166 amphibious vehicles came off the lines. Some 70,000 units by the end of the war. In addition during the war some 1,500 Type VW 60 (KdF) Volkswagens were produced, together with the military Beetle VW 82E (Beetle on jeep-type chassis) and VW 87 (all-wheel-drive Beetle).

At the end of the war, in May 1945, two-thirds of the Volkswagen factory was in ruins. After the British occupation forces had taken over the plant they first set up a provisional repair shop for their own requirements. In order to prevent the threatened demolition they built Volkswagens out of parts stock. As early as March 1946 the 1,000th Type 51 Beetle, a slightly modified military Beetle VW 82E, came off the line, in October the 10,000th.

Most of these vehicles saw servive as CCG cars (Control Commission for Germany).

In 1948 a new era began for the Volkswagen. On 1st January Heinz Nordhoff took over directorship of the ailing Volkswagen factory. He began with the formation of the sales and service network and systematic model updating of the Beetle which was immediately also allowed to be exported and brought in valuable foreign exchange. By 13th May 1949 the 50,000th post-war Beetle came off the line, the 100,000th following in March 1950. It would however take a while to reach the first million, on

Test drive for the press on the occasion of the International Automobile Exhibition in Berlin in February/March 1939.

On a demonstration run through Germany in 1939.

5th April 1955.

By the end of the 50's the Volkswagen factory was one of the biggest motor manufacturers in the world, fourth after three American producers. The Beetle was now exported to more than 140 countries. The biggest customer was the USA.

Dipl.-Ing. Heinz Nordhoff, previously member of the Opel board and during the war head of the then largest European truck factory in Brandenburg, had made a thorough study of the production and sales methods of General Motors at their main works in the USA and knew that even the technically most advanced design could only succeed with the aid of an adequate sales and service organisation.

Therefore in the following years in addition to the construction of production facilities, the testing and development departments, he pressed ahead with the extension of an efficient dealer and workshop organisation, thus laying the foundation for the world-wide success of the Beetle.

The Beetle of that time was not a thing of beauty; badly painted and cobbled together with much improvisation, it also represented an unpleasant remnant of the Nazi period and as such was not much loved, especially by the victors. Nordhoff once described the post war Beetle most accurately: 'a wretched, ugly thing, a car with more defects than a dog has fleas'.

Compared with the earlier models the Beetles of 1950 already showed numerous improvements. In addition to the two Beetle versions, standard and export, the Volkswagen range comprised the 2+2-seater Hebmüller convertible, the four-seater Karmann convertible and the latest product, the Transporter developed from the Beetle. This was internally known as the Type 2 and as a light truck was almost as successful as the Beetle.

The 'wretched, ugly thing' had meanwhile become a serviceable, high quality everyday car that need fear no unfavourable comparison.

In 1953 the hitherto customary split rear window, also known as the pretzel window, was replaced with a somewhat larger oval one. One year later the engine output rose from 25 to 30 bhp.

In 1955 when the millionth Beetle came off the line over 1,500 vehicles per day were being produced. The Beetle was given a new exhaust muffler with twin end-pipes.

1957 saw some important changes, notably a still larger rear window and a completely new dashboard. In 1960 the engine output was again

An early example of the versatility of the Volkswagen: The Berlin-Rome car of 1939. Although built especially for the planned Berlin-Rome Rally, the three aerodynamic sport Volkswagens (VW 64) never fulfilled their intended role, for on the 1st September 1939 the Second World War broke out. Berlin-Rome had to be postponed.

This early Beetle with pick-up body never went into mass production; it was used inside the works as a transporter.

There was also a Beetle delivery van: however, only a handful were built and they too were only intended for service inside the works.

increased, this time by 13 percent to 34 bhp, a sensation at the time.

In the sixties, when the Beetle had become the best selling production car in the world, over a million cars per year were coming off the lines and the Beetle was constantly being improved: flashing turn signals replaced the hitherto customary trafficators in 1960, in 1964 all models were given a larger glass area all-round, in 1965 the engine output was increased to 40 bhp, and from August 1970 to 44 bhp. In the same year a reworked Beetle appeared with larger luggage boot, new running gear with McPherson struts at the front and semi-trailing arm axle at the rear designated Type 1302, or 1302 S with 50 bhp engine.

In 1972 came the VW 1303, actually the same model but with panoramic windscreen and a new dashboard and in this form the last design in the constant development of the Beetle.

By 12th February Beetle production had exceeded that of the Model T Ford with more than 15 million units; barely nine years later the 20-millionth came off the line. So far over 20.6 million Beetles of all types have been produced, a unique record. World-wide there still exist some eight million Beetles; in the Federal Republic alone just under a million are still registered.

Of the 5,115 components which go to make up a complete Beetle only one has remained unchanged throughout its years of maturity: the clamping strip for the bonnet seal.

Members of the workforce pose proudly in front of the first mass produced Beetle ready for delivery in the war year 1941.

The VW Type 87, a Beetle with four wheel drive for the German army, better known under the name „Kommandeurswagen" (Commanding officer's vehicle).

Beetle assembly lines
worldwide

Federal Republic of Germany

1938–1974	Wolfsburg
1964–1978	Emden
1974–1975	Hanover
1965–1969	Ingolstadt
1949–1980	Osnabrück (Convertible)
1957–1976	Australia
1954–1975	Belgium
1953	Brazil
1970–1975 (Import)	Costa Rica
1972–1976	Indonesia
1950–1977 (Import)	Ireland

1973–1976	Yugoslavia
1968–1977 (Import)	Malaysia
1954–	Mexico
1954–1972 (Import)	New Zealand
1975–	Nigeria
1966– (Import)	Peru
1959–1981 (Import)	Philippines
1964–1976 (Import)	Portugal
1968–1974 (Import)	Singapore
1951–1979	South Africa
1972–1974 (Import)	Thailand
1961–1982 (Import)	Uruguay
1963–1981 (Import)	Venezuela

Instead of the planned mass production of KdF cars, it was the Kübelwagen (VW 82), the vehicle designed for all-terrain use, which rolled off the production line in large numbers. By the end of the war some 55 000 had been built.

Necessity is the mother of invention: Because of the acute lack of fuel, experiments were made during the war with Kübelwagens and Beetles equipped with wood gas generators.

One of the best-known Porsche designs based on the Beetle: The amphibian VW 166. By 1944 more than 14 000 had been built.

Im Zeichensaal arbeiten seit Jahren die Konstrukteure immer wieder neue Verbesserungen aus

Den Groß-Glockner nimmt der KdF-Wagen spielend

KdF-Wagen brochure from 1938

Brochures, stamps and post cards

Fahrgestell des KdF-Wagens mit aufmontierten Vordersitzen, von oben gesehen

Der Innenlenker, Preis RM 990.- ab Werk Fallersleben

TECHNISCHE EINZELHEITEN

Das Fahrgestell hat einen durch Stahlbleche abgedeckten Mittelprofilrahmen mit einer hinteren Gabelung zur Aufnahme der Antriebsaggregate (Motor, Kupplung, Getriebe, Differential und Hinterachse). Das Reserverad ist auf dem Rahmenkopf angebracht. Dadurch wird bei etwaigen Zusammenstößen die Gefahr für die Insassen stark herabgesetzt.

Der KdF=Wagen ist mit Warmluftheizung ausgestattet. Die angewärmte Gebläseluft des Motors wird durch Hohlträger in den Fahrgastraum und an die Windschutzscheibe zur Beheizung geführt.

Antrieb:	Auf Hinterräder.
Federung:	Durch verkapselte Drehstabfederung. Jedes Rad ist einzeln aufgehängt (Vollschwingachse).
Schmierung:	Die wenigen Schmierstellen des KdF-Wagens sind mit Schmiernippeln ausgestattet.
Vierradbremse:	Die mechanische Bremse wirkt als Innenbackenbremse auf alle 4 Räder. Die Bremsseile sind im Rahmen geführt und vollkommen geschützt. Die zwischen den Vordersitzen angeordnete Handbremse wirkt ebenfalls auf alle 4 Räder.
Reifengröße:	Vorn und hinten 4,5/16.
Radstand:	2400 mm, Spur: Vorn 1290 mm, hinten 1250 mm.
Bodenfreiheit:	220 mm bei einer Belastung mit 4 Personen zu je 75 kg und etwa 50 kg Gepäck.
Eigengewicht:	650 kg fahrfertig.
Wagenlänge:	4,20 m, Wagenbreite: 1,55 m, Wagenhöhe 1,55 m.
Karosserie:	In Ganzstahlausführung ist der Stromlinienform weitgehend angenähert. Sie bietet bequem Platz für 4 Personen. Selbst auf längeren Reisen können 4 Erwachsene und 1 Kind mit Gepäck gut untergebracht werden.
Lackierung:	Blaugrau.

6

Der Innenlenker mit Faltdach (Cabriolimousine)
Preis: Wegen der höheren Produktionskosten kommt ein Aufschlag von RM 60.- hinzu

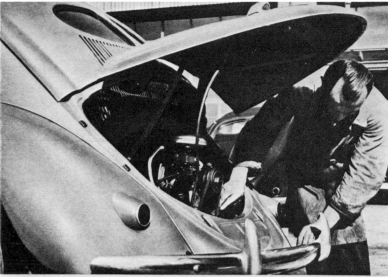

Der Motor im Heck des KdF-Wagens ist gut zugänglich

DER MOTOR DES KDF=WAGENS

Der KdF=Wagen hat einen Vierzylinder=Boxermotor, der im Heck des Wagens untergebracht ist. Die Zylinder arbeiten im Viertakt und haben einen Hubraum von 986 ccm. Bei einer normalen Drehzahl von 3000 p. M. leistet der Wagen 23,5 PS, das entspricht einer Stundengeschwindigkeit von rund 100 km.

Der Motor hat Luftkühlung. Im Luftführungsgehäuse ist der Ölkühler untergebracht, der so bemessen ist, daß niedrige Öltemperaturen auch bei größter Beanspruchung stets für eine ausreichende Schmierung aller Schmierstellen des Motors sorgen. Hierdurch wird die erstaunliche Autobahnfestigkeit des KdF=Wagens erreicht, die Höchstgeschwindigkeit gleich Dauergeschwindigkeit sein läßt. Die Kühlung wird nicht wie bei einem vorn liegenden Motor von der Geschwindigkeit des Fahrzeuges beeinflußt, sondern hängt von der Drehzahl des Motors ab. Dadurch wird in gebirgigem Gelände selbst bei geringer Geschwindigkeit und höchster Motorbeanspruchung eine Überhitzung restlos vermieden.

Ventile:	kopfgesteuert.
Zündung:	Batterie=Lichtmaschinenzündung.
Batterie:	6 Volt.
Lichtmaschine:	spannungsregulierend.
Anlasser:	mit Ritzel auf Schwungrad wirkend.
Vergaser:	Fallstromvergaser.

Kraftstoff=Förderung:	entsprechend den bestehenden Vorschriften sind Motor und Benzintank voneinander getrennt untergebracht. Eine Kraftstoffpumpe fördert das Benzin vom Tank zum Motor.
Kupplung:	Einscheibentrockenkupplung.
Getriebe:	4 Vorwärtsgänge, 1 Rückwärtsgang, 3. und 4. Gang geräuscharm. Die Höchstgeschwindigkeit des 1. Ganges ist 20 km, des 2. Ganges 40 km, des 3. Ganges 65 km in der Stunde.
Ölverbrauch:	normal nur bei Ölwechsel (2,5 Liter für etwa 2500 Kilometer).
Kraftstoff=Verbrauch:	6 bis 7 Liter Benzin auf 100 Kilometer je nach Fahrweise und Gelände.

Der Motor des KdF=Wagens zeichnet sich durch leichte Zugänglichkeit zu seinen Einzelteilen aus. Der Motoraus= und =einbau ist in kürzester Frist durchzuführen, man braucht dazu etwa je 10 Min. Der Motor des KdF=Wagens ist so konstruiert, daß alle Sorten Benzin des In= und Auslandes gefahren werden können.

Und die Reparaturen?
Es werden neuartige Wege beschritten werden, die Ausgaben für Reparaturen, wenn sie notwendig werden sollten, so niedrig wie möglich zu halten. Eine Vereinfachung ist schon dadurch gegeben, daß die einzelnen Teile des KdF=Wagens, auch der Motor, gut zugänglich sind und ebenso leicht montiert werden können. Ferner werden eine ganze Reihe Austauschteile vorbereitet. Bei größeren Unfällen tritt die Versicherung in Kraft.

Der Gangschalter und die Handbremse sind zwischen den Sitzen angeordnet, so daß das Einsteigen von der rechten Wagenseite zum Führersitz ungehindert vor sich gehen kann.

Die breite Tür des KDF=Wagens mit Fensterkurbel und Klinke.

Der Benzintank im Vorderteil des KDF=Wagens faßt 25 Liter ein= schließlich Reserve. Die 3–4 Liter Reservebenzin reichen zu einer Fahr= strecke von rund 50 Kilometern, so daß in jedem Falle eine Tankstelle erreicht werden kann. Davor das Reserverad.

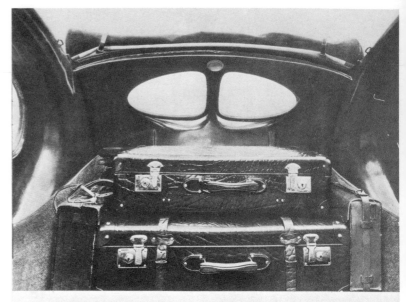

Der Gepäckraum ist beim KDF=Wagen besonders reichlich bemessen. Auch auf längeren Fahrten reicht er für 4 bis 5 Personen vollkommen aus. Hinter den Rücksitzen ist ein Raum für mehrere größere Handkoffer nebst zusätzlichem Kleingepäck wie Schreibmaschine, Grammophon, Badezeug usw. Unter der Vorderhaube können außerdem Rucksäcke, Decken oder ein mittlerer Koffer untergebracht werden.

Alle Fenster sind sehr groß gehalten, auch das Rückfenster, das ebenfalls aus Glas besteht. Über dem Rückfenster befindet sich die Wageninnenbeleuchtung.

Der KDF=Wagen hat einen Doppelscheibenwischer. Der Antrieb liegt verdeckt unterhalb der Windschutzscheibe. Er stört somit nicht das Blickfeld.

Die Schnittzeichnung zeigt die Anordnung aller Sitze
zwischen den Achsen, die reichliche Bemessung der Karosserie und die Unterbringungsmöglichkeiten für Gepäck

FAHREIGENSCHAFTEN

Die große Windschutzscheibe sichert einen guten Straßenüberblick

Bei den grundlegenden Entwürfen für den Aufbau des KDF-Wagens zog der Konstrukteur Dr. Porsche vielfach seine Erfahrungen aus dem Rennwagenbau heran. Obwohl der Vergleich eines vielhundert-pferdigen Rennfahrzeuge, das ausschließlich für die Entwicklung höchster Geschwindigkeiten gebaut ist, mit einem Fahrzeug für den täglichen Gebrauch einer mehrköpfigen Familie auf den ersten Blick sonderbar erscheinen mag, so findet der Techniker doch hier mancherlei Parallele:

Das Gewicht des vollbesetzten KDF-Wagens und das des startbereiten Rennwagens sind nahezu gleich, d. h. um 1000 kg. Radstand und Spur sind beim Rennwagen zwar etwas größer, aber hinsichtlich der Fe-derung und Gewichtsverteilung ergeben sich wertvolle Hinweise der einen Konstruktion auf die andere. Wie es beim Rennwagen von größter Wichtigkeit schien, eine Verschiebung der Gewichtsverteilung zwischen Vorder- und Hinterrädern durch die allmähliche Entleerung des gewaltigen Benzintanks und

deffen rasche Wiederauffüllung zu vermeiden, so war beim KDF-Wa-gen ein ganz ähnliches Problem durch die wechselnde Besetzung mit einer Person oder mit fünf Insassen zu bewältigen.

Dieses Problem wurde dadurch ge-löst, daß beim KDF-Wagen die Sitze im Gegensatz zu den Ausführungen der meisten Wagentypen so weit nach vorn verlegt wurden, daß die Gewichtsverteilung nahezu unver-ändert bleibt, gleichgültig ob der Wagen mit einer oder fünf Personen besetzt ist!

Vorn blieb dann noch genügend Platz für die Unterbringung des Tanks und Reserverads, während der Mo-tor mit Kupplung, Getriebe und Dif-ferential, zu einem Block zusammen-gefaßt, im Heck des Wagens unter-gebracht wurde.

Eine Anordnung der vorgesehenen vier Zylinder in einer Reihe hätte nun aber einen zu langen rückwär-tigen Ausbau ergeben und außerdem die Schwerpunktlage ungünstig be-einflußt. Man griff daher zu der weit kürzeren und leichteren Boxer-An-ordnung, die eine geradezu als ideal zu bezeichnende Gewichtsverteilung von etwa 44 Proz. vorn und 56 Proz. hinten ergibt, die auch der idealen Gewichtsverteilung eines Renn-wagens entspricht.

Als selbstverständlich erschien außer-dem die Konstruktion des KDF-Wa-gens als Vollschwingachser, die sich nicht nur im Rennwagenbau, son-dern auch bei Zehntausenden von deutschen Gebrauchswagen bestens bewährt hatte. Während bei den Vorderrädern hierfür ein parallel in Fahrtrichtung schwingendes System gewählt wurde, ist hinten eine ela-stisch verstrebte Pendelachse vorge-sehen — Schwingachssystem, die sich in nahezu gleicher Ausführung beim Auto-Union-Rennwagen vorfinden. Der Erfolg ist eine ganz ausgezeich-nete Straßenlage. Sie gibt dem Fah-rer auch beim Nehmen scharfer Kurven in hohem Tempo ein außer-ordentliches Gefühl der Sicherheit.

KATSCHBERG

32% STEIGUNG
I. GANG

18% STEIGUNG
II. GANG

9% STEIGUNG
III. GANG

IV. GANG
100 KM.

Das Armaturenbrett ist sehr übersichtlich. Rechts und links zwei Aufbewahrungskästen. Da=
zwischen der Tachometer sowie ein Raum für ein Rundfunkgerät. (Für den KdF=Wagen wird ein Spezial=
rundfunkgerät mit Europaempfang entwickelt.)

Der Tachometer enthält Geschwindigkeitsmesser und Kilometerzähler. Um den Tachometer sind vier
Kontrollämpchen angeordnet: Links oben meldet sich ein rotes Licht, wenn die Ladearbeit der Licht=
maschine aus irgendwelchen Gründen unterbrochen ist. Darunter leuchtet ein grünes Licht auf, wenn
der Öldruck der Motorschmierung nicht ausreicht. Rechts oben zeigt ein gelbrotes Licht die Tätigkeit
der Winker an, und darunter ein blaues, daß die Scheinwerfer auf volles Licht geschaltet sind.

Unterhalb des Tachometers wird mit dem Schlüssel die Zündung eingeschaltet. Links davon der Be=
dienungshebel für die Scheibenwischer, rechts für die Lichtschaltung.

In der Mitte des Armaturenbretts ist unten der Starterknopf und oben der Bedienungshebel für die
Winker angebracht.

Vor dem linken Vordersitz befindet sich das Lenkrad mit eingebautem Signalknopf.

Zur Fußbedienung: Scheinwerferumschaltung, Kupplungs=, Brems= und Gaspedal. Rechts der
Benzinumschalter (Dreiwegehahn).

13

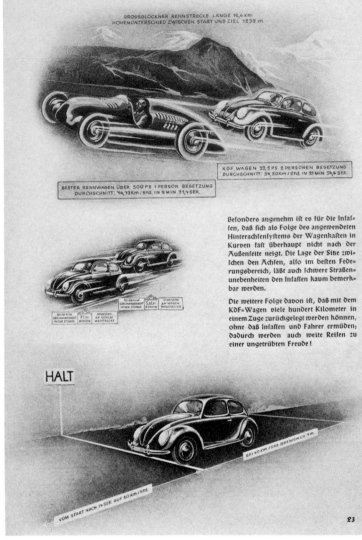

Besonders angenehm ist es für die Insas=
sen, daß sich als Folge des angewendeten
Hinterachsensystems der Wagenkasten in
Kurven fast überhaupt nicht nach der
Außenseite neigt. Die Lage der Sitze zwi=
schen den Achsen, also im besten Fede=
rungsbereich, läßt auch schwere Straßen=
unebenheiten den Insassen kaum bemerk=
bar werden.

Die weitere Folge davon ist, daß mit dem
KdF=Wagen viele hundert Kilometer in
einem Zuge zurückgelegt werden können,
ohne daß Insassen und Fahrer ermüden;
dadurch werden auch weite Reisen zu
einer ungetrübten Freude!

23

30

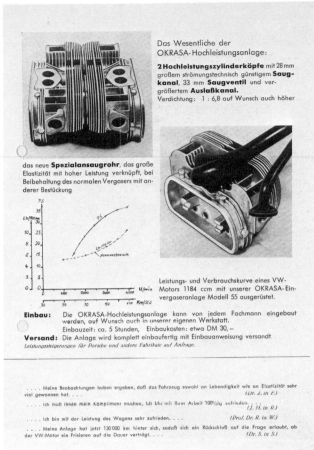

Das Wesentliche der OKRASA-Hochleistungsanlage:

2 Hochleistungszylinderköpfe mit 28 mm großem strömungstechnisch günstigem **Saugkanal**, 33 mm **Saugventil** und vergrößertem **Auslaßkanal**.
Verdichtung: 1 : 6,8 auf Wunsch auch höher

das neue **Spezialansaugrohr**, das große Elastizität mit hoher Leistung verknüpft, bei Beibehaltung des normalen Vergasers mit anderer Bestückung

Leistungs- und Verbrauchskurve eines VW-Motors 1184 ccm mit unserer OKRASA-Einvergaseranlage Modell 55 ausgerüstet.

Einbau: Die OKRASA-Hochleistungsanlage kann von jedem Fachmann eingebaut werden, auf Wunsch auch in unserer eigenen Werkstatt.
Einbauzeit: ca. 5 Stunden, Einbaukosten: etwa DM 30,—

Versand: Die Anlage wird komplett einbaufertig mit Einbauanweisung versandt.

Leistungssteigerungen für Porsche und andere Fabrikate auf Anfrage.

. . . . Meine Beobachtungen haben ergeben, daß das Fahrzeug sowohl an Lebendigkeit wie an Elastizität sehr viel gewonnen hat. . . . (Dr. Z. in P.)

. . . . Ich muß Ihnen mein Kompliment machen, Ich bin mit Ihrer Arbeit 100%ig zufrieden. . . . (J. H. in R.)

. . . . Ich bin mit der Leistung des Wagens sehr zufrieden. . . . (Prof. Dr. R. in W.)

. . . . Meine Anlage hat jetzt 130 000 km hinter sich, sodaß sich ein Rückschluß auf die Frage erlaubt, ob der VW-Motor ein Frisieren auf die Dauer verträgt. . . . (Dr. S. in S.)

Oettinger brochure from 1956

Zehn, zwölf Stunden hintereinander in so einem kleinen Ding sind nicht gerade gemütlich."

DIE „SPIRIT OF SANTA PAULA" FLOG UND FLOG UND FLOG.

Es war ein typisch englischer Wettbewerb: Wer Lust und einen Pilotenschein hatte, sollte versuchen, so schnell wie möglich vom Empire State Building in New York zum Fernsehturm im Herzen von London zu kommen. Den Gewinnern dieses transatlantischen Rennens winkten fette Geldprämien der Londoner Tageszeitung Daily Mail. Das kleinste Flugzeug des Wettbewerbs wurde von einem serienmäßigen VW-1200-Motor angetrieben. Sein Pilot war der gebürtige Tscheche und heutige Düsenjet-Pilot einer amerikanischen Fluggesellschaft, Mira Slowak, 40. Nach einer strapaziösen Reise von 175 Stunden, 42 Minuten und 7,11 Sekunden kam er am Ziel an. Als Sieger seiner Klasse.

Across the Atlantic Ocean with a plane powered by a Beetle engine Mira Slowak and his "Spirit of Santa Paula"

CABRIOLET

Zwei Modelle stehen zur Wahl: das *Standard-* und das *Export-Modell.* Die kostbare Ausstattung des Export-Modells wurde für die unzähligen ausländischen VW-Freunde und für alle diejenigen geschaffen, die auf beachteten Komfort und besonders bequemes Schalten Wert legen. Im übrigen aber gleichen sich beide Modelle vollkommen in bezug auf Motor, Federung, Ganzstahl-Bauweise, Dreischicht-Lackierung in Kunstharz-Emaille, Heizung, Lüftung und vor allem hinsichtlich der sprichwörtlichen Wirtschaftlichkeit des VW.
Mit dem *VW-Cabriolet* (Karmann-Karosserie) hat man

praktisch „Zwei Wagen in einem": das völlig wind- und wetterfeste geschlossene Automobil für kalte Tage (ebenso warm und behaglich wie die Limousine) und den schicken, offenen Sportwagen.
Auch das *Sonnendach* (Bauart Golde) hat viele Freunde gewonnen. Geschlossen bietet es vollkommene Geborgenheit; und offen macht es den VW gewissermaßen zu einer windgeschützten Ecke inmitten der Natur. Hinzu kommt: auch bei schneller Fahrt ist das in jeder Stellung fixierbare VW-Sonnendach mit einem Griff leicht zu öffnen und zu schließen.

SONNEN-DACH

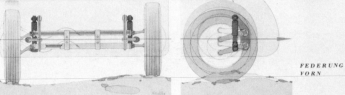

Beim VW ermöglicht — im Gegensatz zu großhaubigen Fahrzeugen — die gedrungene Wölbung des Bugs die Sicht auch unmittelbar vor den Wagen und gibt damit eine Sicherheit des Fahrens, die ohne Beispiel ist

Serienmäßig eingebaute, feinregulierbare Warmluftheizung spendet ausreichend Wärme für das Wageninnere

Zweckmäßig ist auch die innere Architektur des VW. Die Polsterstoffe wie auch die Tür- und Wandverkleidungen harmonieren mit dem neuen Farbsortiment der Lackierung. Sitze und Lehnen sind hinsichtlich weicher Federung und haltbietender Plastik (Randwülste aus Schaumgummi) geradezu ideal konstruiert. Die Vordersessel sind auch während der Fahrt einzeln verstellbar und haben stärker geneigte Lehnen; die breite Sitzbank im Fond bietet erforderlichenfalls drei Personen Platz, denen durch größeren Abstand zwischen Vorder- und Hintersitzen und durch Erweiterung des Fußraumes ausreichende Bewegungsfreiheit geschaffen wurde. In der ebenso modern-geschmackvollen wie technisch durchdachten Armaturentafel vereinigt sich in handlicher Anordnung lückenlos alles, was zum Fahren notwendig oder nützlich ist:

1. WINKERHEBEL an der Lenksäule, von der linken Hand mit einem Finger zu betätigen

2. Großes ZENTRALINSTRUMENT mit Tachometer, Kilometerzähler und den im Zifferblatt harmonisch eingefügten Kontroll-Leuchten für Lichtmaschine und Kühlung (rot), Öldruck (grün), Fernlicht (blau) und Winker (Doppelpfeil)

3. Sehr ansprechendes, überraschend griffiges, hellfarben getöntes ZWEISPEICHENLENKRAD mit schwarz-goldenem, wappengeschmücktem Signalknopf (Export-Modell)

4. Flinke SCHEIBENWISCHER mit weitem Ausschlag und festem Aufdruck, beim Export-Modell mit automatischer Rückkehr in Tiefstellung beim Abschalten

5. Platz für RUNDFUNKSKALA und Bedienungsknöpfe, linksdaneben ein Zugschalter für Scheibenwischer, ferner ein Dreh-Zugschalter für Scheinwerfer und die feinregulierbare Beleuchtung des Zentralinstruments

6. Hinter geschmackvollem Ziergitter der große Raum für den Einbau eines RADIOGERÄTES

7. Handlich rechts vor dem Fahrer der Zugknopf für die LUFTKLAPPE ALS STARTERHILFE

8. Kombiniertes ZÜND-ANLASS-SCHLOSS; Zündschlüssel ist gleichzeitig auch Türschlüssel

9. Versenkbarer, großer KIPP-ASCHER

10. Schließbarer, geräumiger HANDSCHUHKASTEN

Das Problem des Parkens im Großstadtgewühl löst sich beim VW ganz von selbst: seine besondere Wendigkeit, sein geringer Platzbedarf in Länge und Breite gestatten dem Fahrer, ihn mühelos auch in kurze Parklücken einzurangieren

DAS FAHRGESTELL

FEDERUNG VORN

Alle vier Räder des VW sind einzeln aufgehängt und unabhängig voneinander gefedert (Vollschwingachs-Prinzip)

Vorn bergen zwei parallele, miteinander verbundene Querrohre je einen durchgehenden, aus acht Federblättern bestehenden Vierkant-Torsionsstab, dessen Ende

jeweils mit dem dazugehörigen Traghebel verbunden ist. Die Traghebel bilden Parallelogramme, die unter allen Fahrbedingungen eine einwandfreie Federungs-Geometrie und progressiv ansteigende Federkräfte ergeben. Die Spur bleibt beim Durchfedern der Räder auf Unebenheiten unverändert.

FEDERUNG HINTEN

Die Hinterachse besteht aus zwei Pendel-Halbachsen, die ebenfalls unabhängig voneinander durchfedern können. In einem durchgehenden Querrohr befinden sich zwei in Rahmenmitte abgestützte Torsionsstäbe, die, durch Federstreben mit den Halbachsen verbunden, jedes Rad einzeln weich abfedern • Dank dieses fortschrittlichen Federungs-

Systems, das in sich sorgfältig abgestimmt und durch hydraulische Langhub-Teleskop-Stoßdämpfer progressiv gedämpft ist, wird ein Fahrverhalten erreicht, das völlig frei von Nickbewegungen und störendem Nachschwingen bleibt, wie dies vordem gewöhnlich nur bei Fahrzeugen von viel größerem Radstand möglich war.

LENKUNG

Der VW besitzt eine sehr folgsame und präzise Lenkung. Die Anordnung der geteilten Spurstange macht die Lenkung von den Federbewegungen der Vorderräder unabhängig, so daß Fahrbahnstöße vom Lenkrad ferngehalten werden. Die Lenkung geht spielend leicht; aus der Kurvenfahrt kehrt sie selbsttätig in die Geradeaus-Stellung zurück.

Beetle brochure from 1954

1 Reserverad
2 Kraftstoffbehälter
3 Lenkgetriebe
4 Hydraulische, doppelt wirkende Langhub-Teleskop-Stoßdämpfer
5 Traghebel der einzeln aufgehängten Vorderräder
6 Tragrohre mit zwei durchgehenden 6-Blatt-Drehfederstäben
7 Geteilte Spurstange

8 Super-Ballonreifen
9 Hauptbremszylinder der hydraulischen Fußbremse
10 Fußhebelwerk
11 Winkerhebel an der Lenksäule
12 Warmluftzuführung der serienmäßigen Heizung

13 Entfroster-Warmluftdüse
14 Schwenkbare Drehfenster mit Innenverriegelung
15 Drehknopf zur Feineinstellung der Warmluftheizung
16 Batterie getrennt vom Motorraum
17 Tragrohr mit rundem Drehstab auf jeder Seite zur Einzelabfederung der Hinterräder
18 Federstreben

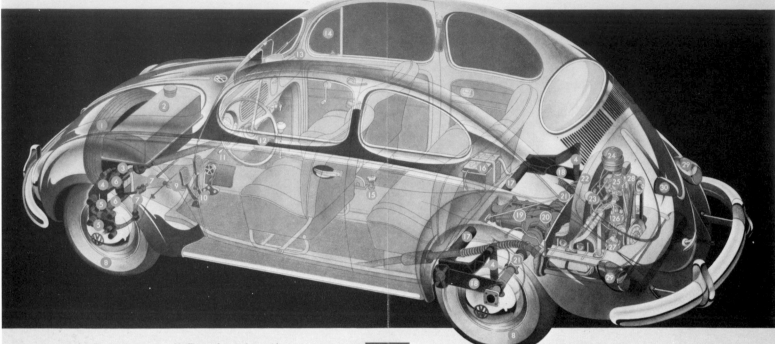

19 Viergang-Sperrsynchrongetriebe
20 Achsantrieb
21 Pendelhalbachsen
22 Kühlgebläse-Gehäuse
23 Zündspule
24 Ölbadluftfilter
25 Solex-Fallstrom-Vergaser mit Beschleunigungspumpe

26 Zündverteiler mit Unterdruckverstellung
27 Kraftstoff-Förderpumpe
28 Lichtmaschine mit Spannungsregler
29 Bremsleuchte kombiniert mit Schlußlichtern und Rückstrahlern
30 Kennzeichen-Leuchte

MOTOR

DER berühmte, in rund dreiviertel Millionen Exemplaren bewährte VW-Motor ist ein luftgekühlter Vierzylinder-Viertakt-Boxermotor mit hängenden Ventilen. Er liegt im Heck des Fahrzeugs und ist am Triebwerkgehäuse, das seinerseits gegen den Wagen isoliert ist, freischwebend angeflanscht. Je zwei Zylinder liegen sich waagerecht gegenüber, wodurch niedrige Schwerpunktlage und beste Raumausnutzung erzielt werden. Als typischer Kurzhuber hat er besonders niedrige Kolbengeschwindigkeiten; daraus erklären sich sein ganz ungewöhnlich geringer Verschleiß, seine absolute Autobahn-Ausdauer und seine sprichwörtliche Langlebigkeit. Die Kurbelwelle dieses Motors ist vierfach gelagert, aus Mangan-Stahl im Gesenk geschmiedet, dynamisch ausgewuchtet und an den Lagerstellen gehärtet. Auf der Kurbelwelle sind die Pleuel in Bleibronzelagern gebettet. Motor, Getriebe, Differential und Hinterachse bilden einen einzigen, organisch gefügten Block, mit dem Ergebnis einer beachtlichen Raum- und Gewichtsersparnis und einer bequem zugänglichen Anordnung an günstigstem Platz.

Hohes Beschleunigungsvermögen!
In 22 sec auf 80 km/h!

Aus dem Stillstand heraus ist der VW jetzt in 7 sec auf 50 km/h, in 17 sec auf 75 km/h und hat nach 22 sec 80 km/h überschritten. In den ungemein günstig übersetzten VW-Getriebe ist der vierte Gang Schongang bei Dauertempo. Der dritte Gang garantiert Elastizität bei temperamentvollem Überholen, in Kurven, auf schwierigen Strecken, im Stadtverkehr und bei sportlicher Fahrweise.

Höchstgeschwindigkeit gleich Dauergeschwindigkeit!
Bei 110 km/h nur 3400 U/min!

Der VW ist absolut autobahnfest; er kann unbekümmert stundenlang auf Höchstgeschwindigkeit (über 110 km/h) gehalten werden. Niedrige Drehzahlen auch bei dieser Höchstbeanspruchung und kurze Kolbenwege halten den Verschleiß minimal und sichern die bekannt hohe Lebensdauer des VW-Motors.

Der VW-Motor
der neuen Bauserie kennt keine Einfahrvorschrift. Man kann ihn vom ersten Kilometer an unbedenklich bis zur Höchstgeschwindigkeit ausfahren. Dies verdankt er der laufenden Verfeinerung und den jüngsten Neuerungen automobilistischer Produktionstechnik.

Favorit im Gebirge!
Steigfähigkeit bis zu 37%!

Die beiden unteren Gänge bewältigen mit souveräner Sicherheit auch die steilsten Paßstraßen Europas. Diese anerkannte Bergfreundigkeit des VW, seine Überlegenheit in endlosen Serpentinen sind ermöglicht durch die Luftkühlung, bei der mit wachsender Drehzahl des Motors die kühlende Wirkung des Luftstroms automatisch so verstärkt, daß eine gesunde Betriebstemperatur stets gesichert bleibt. Hinzu kommt die überlegene Bodenhaftung durch das Motorgewicht über den angetriebenen Hinterrädern.

Die nur 2¼ Liter betragende Ölfüllung des Motors befindet sich in ständigem Umlauf. Dieses Öl wird je fünfmal in jeder Minute durch einen im Strom der Kühlluft stehenden Spezial-Ölkühler gepumpt, solange es kalt ist aber automatisch unter Umgehung des Ölkühlers direkt zu den Schmierstellen des Motors geführt. Durch den Ölkühler ist die Betriebssicherheit des Motors (wie bei teuren Sportwagen), insbesondere bei lang andauernden Höchstleistungen — bei Autobahn-Dauerfahrten und langen Steigungen — unter allen Temperatur-Verhältnissen gewährleistet.

GEKÜHLTES ÖL

LUFTKÜHLUNG

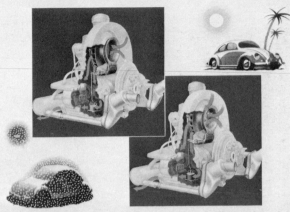

Es ist die Luftkühlung des Motors, die den VW für arktische Kälte, tropische Hitze und alle klimatischen Zwischenstufen gleichermaßen prädestiniert. Luft gefriert nicht, und Luft siedet nicht, und sie bannt die Temperatur des Kühlmittels nicht künstlich unter die Grenze von 100° C, die nur durch den Siedepunkt des Wassers, nicht aber durch den Motor geboten war, dessen gesamter Arbeitsprozeß viel höhere Temperaturen verlangt. Die Luftkühlung des VW-Motors arbeitet progressiv, d. h. ihre Wirkung wächst automatisch mit höherer Drehzahl. 500 Liter Luft durchjagen in jeder Sekunde das einzigartige Kühlsystem des VW-Motors — frei von den vielerlei Anfälligkeiten der Aggregate einer Wasserkühlung. Durch die thermostatische Regelung wird die Menge des Luftstromes je nach Bedarf automatisch gedämmt oder freigegeben, die Erwärmung des Motors auf seine günstigste Betriebs-Temperatur sehr rasch herbeigeführt und eine Unterkühlung bei Fahrten mit gedrosseltem Motor (in der Stadt oder bei anhaltendem Gefälle) sicher vermieden. Ohne jeden Zweifel ist die Luftkühlung ein entscheidend wichtiger und unersetzbarer Faktor für die beispiellose Lebensdauer dieses Motors.

GETRIEBE

Das Synchrongetriebe der Export-Limousine arbeitet durch schrägverzahnte, ständig miteinander im Eingriff befindliche Zahnräder und Kegel-Synchronisierung mit Gleichlauf-Sperren des zweiten, dritten und vierten Gangs wohltuend weich und leise. Der Schaltvorgang vollzieht sich spielend leicht und schnell. Gegenüber dem zwar nicht synchronisierten, aber ebenso zuverlässigen Wechselgetriebe des Standard-Modells stellt das Synchrongetriebe einen Vorsprung an Bequemlichkeit und eine artige Verbeugung vor dem zarten Geschlecht dar.

VERGASER

Ein Solex-Fallstrom-Vergaser mit Beschleunigungspumpe sichert gute Übergänge, temperamentvolle Beschleunigung, geringen Verbrauch und hohe Elastizität des Motors. Auch bei extrem niedrigen Temperaturen springt der Motor sicher an; die Kaltstart-Luftklappe ist mit der Drosselklappe zur progressiven Leerlauferhöhung gekoppelt.

The Beetle Phenomenon
1937 – 1977

1937 Volkswagen Prototype

Max speed: 62 mph (100 kph)

Rear hinged doors

No bumpers
Tyre size: 4.50-16
Brakes: cable operated

Horizontally-opposed,
air cooled engine 985cc
5.6:1 compression ratio
Power: 23.5 bhp DIN at
3,000 rpm

No rear window

Rear View
Volkswagen
Prototype.
1937

1977 Volkswagen Beetle (1200)

Rear window (1938)
Front hood release
inside car (1949)
Hydraulic brakes
(1950)
Swivelling
quarterlights (1952)

5.60 × 15 tyres (1952)
Rear window centre pillar
disappears (1953)
Flashing indicators
introduced (1955)
Double tailpipes (1956)

Rear window enlarged (1958)
Automatic choke
introduced (1961)

Windows enlarged (1965)
Dual braking circuit (1967)
12 volt electrical system (1967)
External tank filler (1968)
"Eurobumpers" (1968)
Heated rear window (1969)
Through flow
ventilation (1971)
Enlarged foil
light cluster
(1972)

Rear View
1977
Volkswagen Beetle.

It took a man like Porsche to invent a car like the Beetle

Ferdinand Porsche was the archetypal 'eccentric inventor'. A diminutive, irascible Austrian, his even looked the part in his baggy tweed suit, steel-rimmed spectacles, and outsize gaffing cap. With no formal engineering training, he was simply a born inventor. As early as 1900, he'd designed a revolutionary transmission system for electric cars, comprising of four electric motors, placed inside the hub of each wheel, eliminating belts and chain drives completely. It won him a Grand Prize at the Paris Universal Exposition of 1900.

In 1906, Porsche, already famous, took over as technical director of Austro-Daimler. His colleagues were immediately struck by his passion for cars and engines.

"As contemporaries observed they could see his eyes grow brighter as he listened to the purr or roar of his creations, making mental notes of what had to be activated, changed or redesigned..."

1936. Adolph Hitler, impressed by Porsche's 16 cylinder, 250 mph Auto Union racing car, took an interest in the Volkswagen (from a propaganda point of view of course). Hoping to win support by making a mass produced car for the German man in the street he discussed a Volkswagen factory—shy at Wolfsburg. And in keeping with his penchant for slogans, he re-named the Kraft du Freude or 'Strength through Joy' car.

So that the poorly paid German working man could afford the car (when it was finally produced), Hitler instituted a special savings scheme. Thousands of Germans put by millions of Marks towards their VWs. But by 1939 and the outbreak of war, not one VW had been sold to the public.

1939-1945. The Wolfsburg plant is turned over to the production of war materials, the famous Kubelwagen and over a million small stoves to warm troops on the Russian front.

1945. The British Army takes over the bombed out Wolfsburg plant. By bolstering low raw materials, they manage to get production of the Beetle going... for the first time. Attempts to interest the British motor industry in the Beetle fail. Nobody can see the potential of this strange vehicle.

The reason for that shape

Ferdinand Porsche wasn't a car designer who aped a 'stylist'. He was an inventor of the Ford Motor Company when and all

Ferdinand Porsche
The Creator
of the Beetle
1875-1951.

What people have said about it

"Mr Ford, I don't think what we can believe it here is worth a damn"... Ernest Breech, Chairman of the Ford Motor Company when

What people have done with it

The first 'Customised' Beetle was the Kubelwagen (literally 'bucket wagon'). Germany's answer to the jeep. But owing to its design as a Porsche's design, what an answer!

The ultra-light weight, plus good traction from the rear engine, allowed it to scamper through deep mud, while everything else was bogged down. Air cooling meant it didn't overheat in the North African desert or freeze up on the Russian Front. Facts which made one Kubelwagen worth 3 jeeps on the black market, after the war. VW also built an amphibious version (able to sealed body, propeller and snorkel exhaust). It proved so seaworthy that it was actually rowed green navigation lights was suggested.

More recently Beetles offering has become a world wide craze.

Originating in South Africa in '65 when somebody removed a Beetle body and replaced it with an open glass fibre tub, calling the result a dune buggy. Here are some of the wilder examples of current Beetle customising.

Water Beetles

The Beetle has taken to the water intentionally and otherwise and taped well. Three years ago a Beetle with special sealing and hollow fuel tanks, called 'The Yellow Submarine' completed the 32 miles from Germany on the Isle of Man to St Bees' head on the Cumberland coast in 7½ hours, in a force 6 gale, pounded by heavy seas.

In June 1971, a Beetle took but an hour to make the ½ mile crossing of Loch Ness. Whilst in an attempt on the Channel Crossing the only reason for failure was the driver's seasickness.

In 1965, in Africa, a newly-wed couple were swept down river in their Beetle, during a storm. They travelled 1000 yards before they were caught by overhanging branches. After 4½ hours, they were winched out by a local farmer! Damage: 1 smell dent in the running board. Again in Africa, the vehicle Gerber family, travelling in an enormous gorge crossing a river when they were swept off the bridge and carried downstream. Mr Gerben managed to climb out through a window and tried to drag the car to the bank. But he lost his hold and watched in horror as his wife and family, frantically rowing 900 yards from a tractor had pulled the car ashore, the Gerbers climbed aboard, and continued their journey.

Flying Beetles

Builders of light aircraft quickly realised that Porsche's lightweight flat four engine, constructed of magnesium alloy and aluminium, was already a ready made aero engine. At present, there are about 9 makes of aircraft flying with slightly modified Beetle engines. Usually the only 'mod' required is a special carburettor for high altitudes and takeoff.

Desert Beetles

Three Australians once drove a Beetle across the South Australian Stony Desert, one of the hottest, harshest places on earth. It survived through temperatures of up to 130 and 140 degrees in the sun picking its way over rocks the size of footballs. Hans Kreis of South West Africa drove his ageing Beetle loaded with 1000 lbs of equipment 1600 miles along the drifting dunes of the notorious Skeleton Coast, and later through the Kalahari Desert. The only mishaps: two punctures.

How Britain got the Bug

The Beetle's entry into Britain in 1953 wasn't easy. Firstly, people were reluctant to have anything to do with what they considered an 'enemy car'. Secondly, a successful small car industry already existed in the UK and in order to compete Volkswagen had to battle uphill all the way. But in spite of early difficulties the Beetle sold. In 1953 sales were 945. By 1959 they'd risen to 10,000 and today 200,000,000 (approx).

'Herbie' - America's Love Bug

In 1969 a new star was introduced to the glamorous world of films. His name Herbie, hero of 'The Love Bug' and 'Herbie rides again' a Beetle with a big heart whose red, white and blue racing stripes made him world famous almost overnight.

"We needed a small car for 'The Love Bug' but we didn't know what sort. So we lined some up in front of the Animation building at the studio... as the employees passed by and on the way to lunch, they all looked at them. They would kick the tyres, turn the steering wheels, or even reach in and sound the horn. But everyone who went by sort of patted the Volkswagen which they adored and one or two even went up to it and talked to it!" the VW had a personality of its own people. Thus we found our star.

40 Years After

The Beetle's broken just about every record going. It's sold more than any other car (19,000,000 to date). It's had a longer production run than any other car (40 years in fact). It's been exported to more countries

Customised Beetles,
even ploughing Beetles.

Snow Beetles
A famous television commercial showed a Beetle coasting through a

1977 Volkswagen Beetle.

1969 Herbie – "The Love Bug."

Rear light cluster development:

1937	1961	1967	1972

1940. The people's Car.

1977 Cabriolet Beetle.

A Flying Beetle/The Fournier Single Seater.

The Beetle's 4 cylinder horizontally opposed air cooled engine.

Schwimmwagen. The first sea-going Beetle.

"The Yellow Submarine" driven by Malc Buchanan, Bill Helin and Roger Ratcliff in June 1973.

The world famous advertising from the 1960s.

A Volkswagen, obviously.

Ugly is only skin-deep.

Some shapes are hard to improve on.

Nobody's perfect.

Is the economy trying to tell you something?

Preisliste

Personenwagen

VW-LIMOUSINE (Standard-Modell)	
serienmäßig lackiert	**DM 3 790**
grundiert	DM 3 745
Mehrpreis für Sonnendach (Bauart GOLDE)	DM 250
VW-LIMOUSINE (Export-Modell)	
serienmäßig lackiert	**DM 4 600**
grundiert	DM 4 555
Mehrpreis für Sonnendach (Bauart GOLDE)	DM 250
VW-CABRIOLET viersitzig	**DM 5 990**
je nach Wunsch Kunstleder- od. Stoffpolsterung — Mehrpreis für Sonderausstattungen (einschließl. Sonderlackierung) auf Anfrage	
KARMANN-GHIA-COUPÉ	**DM 7 500**
(auf VW-Chassis Export-Modell) je nach Wunsch Kunstleder oder Stoffpolsterung, serienmäßig lackiert	

Transporter

VW-PRITSCHENWAGEN „PICK UP"	
serienmäßig lackiert	**DM 5 725**
grundiert	DM 5 655
Mehrpreis für Spriegel und Plane	DM 250
VW-KASTENWAGEN	
serienmäßig lackiert	**DM 5 975**
grundiert	DM 5 885
Mehrpreis für Flügeltüren beidseitig . . .	DM 250

1955 price list

Beetle postcards

Beetle postage stamps and day of first issue stamp (Briefmarken Sieger)

38

Der grosse Tag...
endlich VW-Besitzer

¡Vaya por Dios! Otro golpe de mala suerte.
Pero no se enfade usted, porque no resolverá nada.
Y, al menos, sabe usted que cuenta con los repuestos
originales que necesite a precios absolutamente asequibles.

REPUESTOS
VW
LEGITIMOS

¡que sean **VW** es lo
importante!

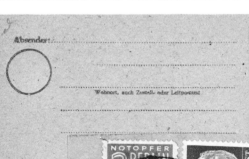

Postkarte

KdF-Wagen

Als der Volkswagen noch KdF-Wagen (,,Kraft
durch Freude'') hieß: Werbemarke von 1939

Beetle production in assembly line

Beetle wedding. Bodywork and chassis are joined together

BEETLE PRODUCTION 1948

1950: One Beetle every three minutes

Out of the Ashes

The Volkswagen works under British administration

Major Ivan Hirst was responsible for the Beetle project at that time and he got production rolling again.

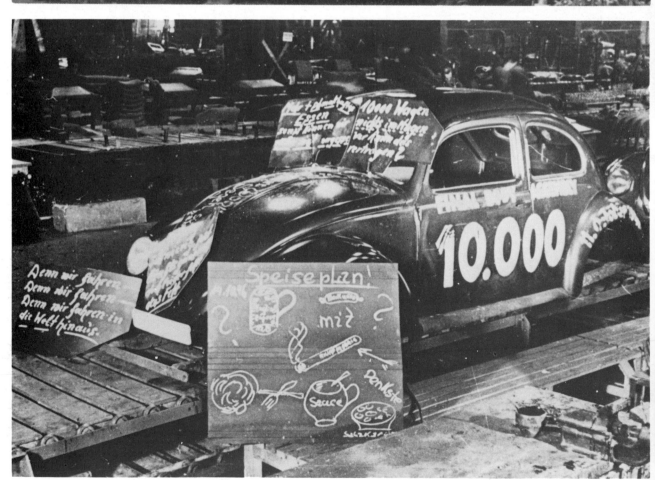

The 1000th VOLKSWAGEN
built during MARCH 1946 coming from Assembly Line

March 1946: The one thousandth Beetle

October 1946: The ten thousandth Beetle

42

BEETLE IN EARLY POST-WAR YEARS

as ambulance with built-in stretcher

as towing vehicle with shortened wheelbase

as service vehicle

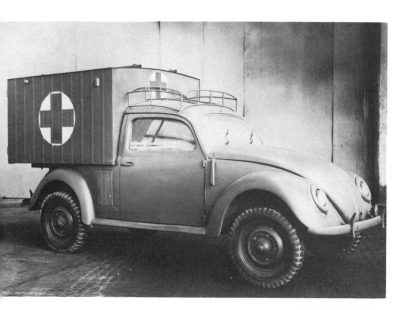

with van body for the Red Cross and for the Post Office

THE BEETLE IS EXPORTED: The Pon brothers from Amersfoort in the Netherlands collected the first 56 saloons in October 1947.

Custom built: Convertible with two windows for Colonel Radclyffe

One-off: Hebmüller-Coupé

Prototype: Hebmüller convertible

44   *Beetle in four-door version, 1952*

POLICE CONVERTIBLES *by Hebmüller*

by Papler ▲▼ *by Austro-Tatra*

Beetle as air-traffic controller 45

Production convertibles by Karmann

Beetle-borne VIPs: Federal Chancellor Konrad Adenauer (left) and general manager Heinz Nordhoff, 1955

The police drove Beetles, too. This is the last patrol car of the Mainz police force; it was taken out of service in 1979.

Today, some Beetles are still in service here and there with the Post Office.

Original KAMEI 1953 Beetle with "depth control"

KAMEI 1975 Beetle with state of the art accessories

Below, left: Veteran Beetle as service vehicle

Below, right: Beetle undergoing crash test

Shelf beneath the dashboard

Tray for cigarettes and matches

Company founder Karl Meier in his 1953 Beetle with arm rest, head restraint and reclining seat

IN-CAR CREATURE COMFORT FROM KAMEI

Footrest and accelerator pedal running plate

Security shelf with safe and flower vase

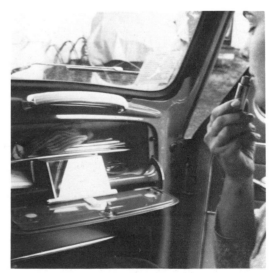

Glove compartment inset with make-up mirror

The "millionth" Beetle

◁ 5th August 1955   ▷ 15th September 1965

◁ 4th December 1961   ▷ 17th February 1972

▷ 15th May 1981

Beetle Summary

Over the decades, the Beetle has hardly changed its appearance at all – the basic technical concept has also remained the same up to today. Nevertheless there is probably no other mass-produced car which has been so thoroughly updated. Year by year it has been improved. Of the 5,115 parts which comprise a Beetle, only one has remained unchanged up to now – the clamping strip for the bonnet seal.

1938

For years previously the various Beetle prototypes had been driven and tested but the Beetle was first presented to the public in 1938 at the Berlin Motor Show.

1946

During the war the VWs built were mainly for military purposes. After the war, however, they really started up in earnest. The British occupation forces were in charge initially.

1949

The early Beetle models which had really Spartan equipment were retained as standard models. Under Nordhoff's direction, the Export model with improved equipment and chrome trim came onto the

1950

Intensive model improvements began. The Export Beetle was fitted with hydraulic brakes; recesses in the side windows at the front to improve ventilation; and, for 250 Marks, with a sliding roof.

1951

The Beetle was equipped with side ventilation flaps, however only for a year – the 'rheumatism flaps' were not a success.

1952

A year of surprises: 15 instead of 16 inch wheels; synchromesh gearbox (Export models only); door windows fitted with opening quarter-lights.

1952

For the last time Beetles had a divided rear windscreen. Instead of only one brake light, two tiny brake lights were incorporated in the rear light units.

1953

The central dividing rib in the rear window disappeared. It was also possible to fit the oval rear windscreen on older models as a service installation.

1955

Engine output had been raised from 24 to 30 bhp in the previous year. A dual exhaust was added this year.

1956

In the meantime the sliding roof was made of weatherproof PVC. Tubeless tyres were introduced – absolutely sensational at the time.

1957

A drastic change: both front and rear windscreens were enlarged. The roller-type accelerator pedal was replaced by a flat one.

1959

Fixed door handles with pushbuttons were introduced on the Beetle, also a foot support for the front passenger and a stabiliser on the front axle.

1960

The engine output increased to 34 bhp. The choke was replaced by an automatic starter on the carburettor. Other changes: asymmetric headlights, turn signals synchromesh for first gear and a steering

1961

Changes were again made this year: steering lock, anchorages for seat belts and a fuel gauge.

1963

A steel sliding roof replaced the PVC sliding roof, for the additional charge of 250 Marks.

1965

The VW 1300 with enlarged windows, 40 bhp and flat hubcaps. The 34 bhp engine only for the standard Beetle.

1966

Another new model: the VW 1500 with 44 bhp. The Beetle was given a wider rear axle and the 1300 and 1600 models had in addition an anti-roll spring.

1967

The Beetle changes its appearance: vertically placed headlights (only on models with higher engine capacity), box-section bumpers, 12 volt electrical system and, for 465 Marks, an automatic gearbox.

1970

A new Beetle with new running gear. The VW 1302 has suspension struts at the front and a double-jointed axle at the rear as on the Automatic Beetle. The S version has 1600 cc and 50 bhp.

1971

Through-flow ventilation was introduced in the previous year with crescent-shaped air outlets behind the side windows. This year ventilation is improved with additional air inlets in engine lid.

1972

The evolution of the Beetle reaches its climax: the VW 1303 with panorama windscreen and new dashboard succeeds the VW 1302. The small body version is retained as the VW 1200.

1974

The 1303 is also improved – the turn signals are integrated in the bumpers. The GOLF arrives. The last Beetle leaves the assembly line at Wolfsburg on 1st July 1974.

1975

As a result of the oil crisis, the demand for the Beetle increases. The 'economy Beetle' is brought out – a 1200 Beetle with Spartan fittings.

1978

The last German Beetle leaves the assembly line at Emden on 18th January. Its production number is 16 255 500. Beetles now come from Mexico.

Beetle inter-national

Ready to be shipped abroad: Since 1978 Beetles travelling the roads of Europe have been produced exclusively in Mexico.

Beetle parade in front of the backdrop of the Volkswagen works: On the left two 1938 VW 38, in the middle the one millionth Beetle of 1955, beside it the 1965 export saloon and the 1976 basic Beetle.

*1986 Beetle
Roadster à la
Hebmüller by
Philipp Eller*

*Beetle as
speedster by
"Speedster
Cabrio Design"
(Ostermann)*

Today a sought-after rarity: 1949 Hebmüller Beetle

Luxurious but not elaborate: dashboard in Hebmüller Beetle

Volks-Royce or Rolls-Wagen?

Beetle convertible with wide tires, flared wheel arches and modified engine by KERSCHER

Topless Beetle: convertible by Eller

DIY Topless Beetle

Beetle with individual styling – but still a Beetle. A French Beetle fan has converted his VW 1302 with a great deal of loving care and attention to detail.

Beetles and convertibles got together to form the longest Beetle queue in the world. The result: 2622 meters of Beetle and an entry in the "Guinness Book of Records".

INDIVIDUALITY IS TOPS

either as split-screen saloon (top, left)
. . . with oversized rear spoiler
. . . in pretzel-window look (bottom)
. . . or as show attraction (right)

Beetle 'M-EX 300' by MAHAG in Munich

TDE Beetles (VW 1302 and 1303) with modified engines by Theo Decker

The version with the Oettinger engine is both pretty and pretty rare, too

Street scene in Ouro Preto in Brazil

△

in a village in Nigeria

◁

Street scene in Cusco/Peru

and just about everywhere ▷

◁

on the sugar plantation in Brazil

▽ *as hunting vehicle in Nigeria*

The police value the Beetle, too, here in Brazil

Road patrol Beetle: As "Yellow angel" of the ADAC (Federal German Automobile Club)

The Beetle worldwide

Impression from Afrika. The Beetle is prized not only in Uganda.

Below left: Painstaking work: hand-carved Beetle in Nigeria.

Right: Beetles have been assembled in Nigeria since 1975. The components required are shipped from Brazil. Of course, "normal" Beetles are produced as well as this hunting vehicle.

Lonely Beetle in front of a church in the Lebanon.

These Beetles are in use with the traffic police in Port Elizabeth/South Africa.

In South Africa production of Beetles ceased on 18th January 1979.

Beetle **250 000** Kewer

Beetle as wedding car in Puebla/Mexico . . .

. . . with the appropriate music

Beetle – assembled in Indonesia

Alongside Mexico, Brazil is today one of the main Beetle producers.

Between October 1950 and January 1951, the Belgian Beetle importer P. D'Ieteren and three companions took a Beetle and a VW bus on an expedition from Brussels to the Congo – they covered some 25 000 kilometers. The Beetle coped easily with difficult terrain, in this case a ford.

The Beetle is also popular in Scandinavia: In Denmark, where delivery began in 1948, the 25 000th Beetle was supplied already in 1956; the souvenir photograph was taken in front of the City Hall in Copenhagen.

In Sweden the name for the Beetle is „Elk's Lip".

Versatile: Beetle as haywagon and mower

Lonely Beetle at the foot of the Matterhorn in Switzerland.

The first and the last Beetles registered in Switzerland, together on 31th March 1983. On the left the first Beetle, built in 1948, on the right the last Beetle. The number plate also records the total number of Beetles imported by the AMAG.

Beetle and Formula V. Many components are identical and even interchangeable.

Prominent Formula V driver: Carl Gustav XVI of Sweden. Anton Konrad (left), today responsible for Public Relations at VW, is giving instructions.

Beetle as lottery prize. For 5 Marks, the price of a ticket, as the prize in the First TV lottery of the Federal Republic of Germany „A Place in the Sun".

It remained a one-off: Maxi-Beetle. Today, it can be seen in the Wolfsburg AutoMuseum.

All you need is a good idea. At Autohaus Nordstadt in Hannover they always have a new stunt up their sleeve. This Beetle is full of water, it is absolutely watertight and has a diver at the wheel.

80

Wolf in sheep's clothing: Carrera Beetle from Nordstadt. Running gear from VW-Porsche, engine from Porsche Carrera, bodywork from VW 1303. The result: 213 km/h top speed.

Dieter Götting in the 160 bhp. Beetle in Zolder.

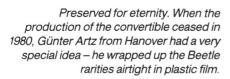

Preserved for eternity. When the production of the convertible ceased in 1980, Günter Artz from Hanover had a very special idea – he wrapped up the Beetle rarities airtight in plastic film.

Maxi Beetle carries twelve
plus 'cox'

With 21 recruits on board

In earlier years it was considered an extraordinary achievement when a car covered 100 000 kilometers and more. Beetle drivers who reached the 100 000 kilometer mark without serious mechanical problem were presented with gold watches, certificates, badges and plaques by the Volkswagen company. By the time the scheme was suspended in 1961, honours and watches had been conferred on more than 160 000 Beetle drivers.

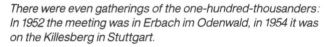

There were even gatherings of the one-hundred-thousanders: In 1952 the meeting was in Erbach im Odenwald, in 1954 it was on the Killesberg in Stuttgart.

24 PS

Diesel engine in the Beetle

Beetle Engines

Modified Beetle engines from 90 to 300 bhp based on Type 1 (Beetle) or Type 4 (VW 411) and, if even more power is needed for the daily run, then even with GTI engine (bottom centre) or six cylinder Porsche powerplant above.

34 PS

Flat twin water-cooled engine

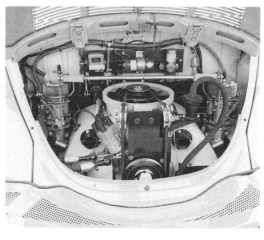
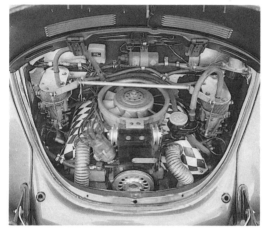
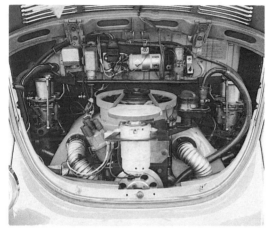

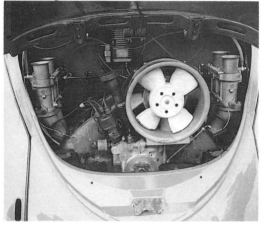

On the VW proving ground in Ehra-Lessien

Beetle and Sport

Spa – Sofia – Lüttich Rally

In Sweden, and not only there, the Beetle is also very popular as a rally-cross vehicle.

In the Benelux Countries as well, the merits of the Rally-cross Beetle are known and appreciated.

In Brazil, specially prepared Beetles are the stars of the national circuit races.

Beetle in the 1985 Paris –
Dakar Rally . . .

Fly Beetle fly! In the course of the 1973 rally
season, the Beetle (VW 1302 S) prepared by
Volkswagen – Porsche of Salzburg became
the terror of race favorites.

. . . and 4000 kilometers
▽ through New Caledonia

"Yellow-black Racer", *a special series of the VW 1303 S with sport accessories*

Also popular as Rally-cross Beetle

With a will of its own: "Nutrocker" from England

◁ △

Rally-cross races in Scandinavia

The Beetle as dragster: At the 'Beetle Meet' in Hanau-Erlensee. – Above, right: with plastic bodywork, tubular space frame and nearly 400 bhp: opposite: as classic (Beetle) dragster

Dragster Beetle today

Filigree work: Front end of drag Beetle

American dragster legend: EMPI
"Inch Pincher" of the sixties

„Redrunner" 1985 ▷

Beetle as boat trailer in the USA

. . . taking part in the Carnival in Mainz

. . . as pick-up Beetle

Beetle as tractor

. . . as snowplough at OETTINGER

GLOW BEETLE
It glows and glows and glows . . .
Eric Staller a New York architect and photographer changed his beetle by means of 1659 electric bulbs and a computer into a glittering thing that can sparkle into the most various light patterns desired. A generator which has been installed instead of the rear seat provides for the necessary electricity. Staller invested five months of labour and approximately 20 000 Dollar in his rolling Beetle light game.

Beetle and Art

"Käfer am Waldrand" by Bernd Schwering (Roth Händle Edition)

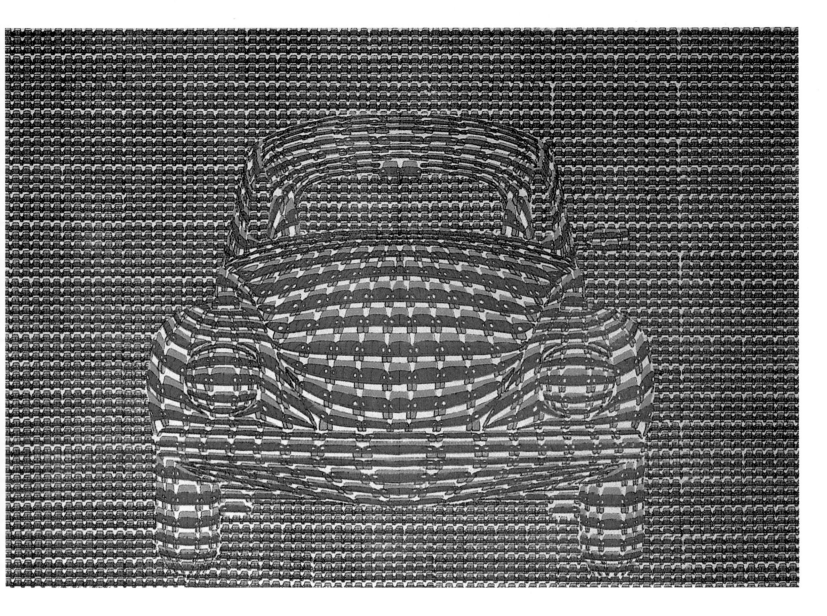

Beetle as printed graphics by Thomas Bayrle

The following Beetle drawings are from Walter Gotschke.

Ferdinand Porsche surrounded by his employees in the yard of the Porsche villa in Stuttgart. The experimental Beetles are V1 and V2 (left front and rear), the third (in the background) is one of the VW 3 series.

A similar scene, this time however, 1946 in Wolfsburg

Traffic as usual in the Königstraße in Stuttgart

Beetles in the USA (New York)

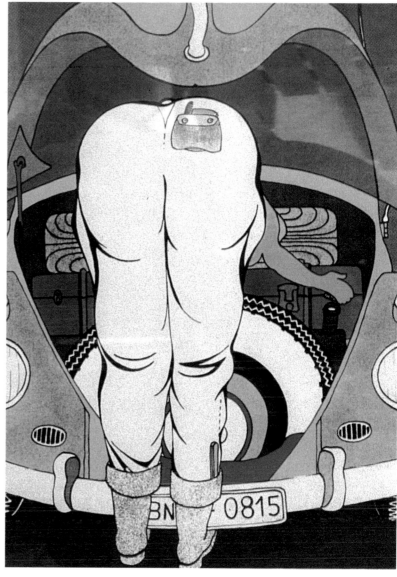

Beetles in art: "Shortened" by J. Dodd

. . . as "Moloch Auto"

◁

Above: "Neubeginn" is the name which the Swede Sune Envall gives his Beetle serigraphy (Galerie Auto & Kunst)

Below: "Private Parking" by Don Eddy

Beetle as Pop Art by Tom Wesselmann

BEETLE MAGAZINES: Throughout the world there is a whole range of more or less well-known automobile journals that concern themselves almost solely with the Beetle. The oldest magazine is the GUTE FAHRT which is published in Germany (first published 1950).

DAS
BREZELFENSTER
CLUBZEITUNG
DER VW-VETERANEN-FREUNDE

Nr. 1/81

Urkäfer

1/81

Gute Fahrt
junior

nederlandse vw brillen vereniging

1953

brillen

BEETLING

VOLKSWAGEN news-sport-tuning-maintenance
Forty Pence

279 JULY, 1981

20 MILLION !

Gute Fahrt
Die Zeitschrift für den Volkswagenfahrer
3/62
DM 1.50

RALLYE MONTE CARLO
S-HH 649

SEPTEMBER 1983 70p

1st Anniversary Issue
VOLKSWAGEN AUDI CAR
AUDI VOLKSWAGEN AUDI VOLKSWAGEN AUDI VOLKSWAGEN

VW Action '83
PREVIEW

OCTOBER 1981 30p

SAFER
VOLKSWAGEN
MOTORING

The INDEPENDENT pro-British magaz
that concentrates on the VW/Audi Fan

TESTING THE TURBO SCIROCCO!
VOLKSWAGE Gre

PORSCHES:
356 HOLIDAY · CUSTOM 914
CARRERA 2000GS!

SPECIAL:
SHOW-
WINNING
CHOPPED-TOP
BEETLES!

HOT ROD HOW TO LOCATE COLLECTIBLE VW
VOLKSWAGE class

Drive Test

$2.50

erglass FIER

THE
OUTSTANDING
JETTA GLI

Sensational St

HOW-TOS:
• Water-Cooled Hop-Up
• Interior Makeovers
• Rebuilding Type IIIs
• Adjustable
I-Beams

RABBIT GTI TURBO ENGINE TEST
VW PORSCHE
APRIL 1985 $2.00

TESTING—
PROJECT 914's KILLER ENGINE
• BEETLE SUSPENSION TRICKS
• RABBIT/SCIROCCO PARTS

VROOM

550-
HP
STREET
BEETLE!

FIRST LOOK: '85 PORSCHE 944 TURBO

ULTIMATE PORSCHE- $90,000 RINSPEED 939

GABRIELLE D'IETEREN ET CHARLOTTE VAN MARCKE DE LUMMEN

DEUX FEMMES AU VOLANT

27146

20. — *Les sourires de la victoire..*
Photo Cape Argus.

In 1951 the Belgians Gabrielle D'Ieteren and Charlotte van Marcke de Lummen took part in a Beetle in a rally right across the African continent from the Mediterranean to Cape Town. They came first in their class.

Das neue VW-Zentrum in USA in Englewood Cliffs, das New York gegenüber am anderen Ufer des Hudson liegt.

Der Automobilmarkt der USA, der bei weitem größte in der Welt mit der leistungsfähigsten Automobilindustrie dieser Erde und mit einem Automobilbestand von über 70 Millionen Wagen, hat von allen nichtamerikanischen Automobilen nur den Volkswagen in beispielloser Weise anerkannt und akzeptiert. Der millionste Volkswagen, der vor kurzem in den USA zugelassen wurde, ist ein erster Markstein in einer großartigen und einmaligen Entwicklung.

An der Spitze der amerikanischen VW-Organisation, die heute 15 Großhändler und 670 Händler zählt, steht die Volkswagen of America, Inc., eine Tochtergesellschaft unseres Unternehmens. VW-Generaldirektor Prof. Dr. Nordhoff übergab im Oktober das neue VW-Verwaltungsgebäude in Englewood Cliffs, New Jersey, der Bestimmung. Die Errichtung dieses VW-Zentrums wird in den USA als Zeichen des Vertrauens gewertet, mit dem das Volkswagenwerk seine Zukunft auf dem amerikanischen Markt sieht.

„Heute wird ein Fünftel der gesamten Volkswagen-Produktion nach den Vereinigten Staaten geliefert: jede Woche wird eine volle Tagesproduktion von rund 5000 Fahrzeugen nach dort verschifft", betonte Professor Nordhoff bei der Einweihung des VW-Zentrums.

Als erster erhält der VW-Generaldirektor das Teilnehmerabzeichen bei der VW-Händlerkonferenz; der General-Manager der Volkswagen of America, Dr. C. H. Hahn (Mitte), ist der nächste.

Excerpt of the 1961 Christmas letter to the shareholders:

On the small picture VW General Director Nordhoff, in the center former General Manager of "Volkswagen of Amerika" Carl Hahn. On January 5, 1959 VW boss Nordhoff had appointed his former assistant boss of "Volkswagen of America". Hahn, at present Chairman of the Board of Volkswagen AG was 32 years young back then.

Wie Sie Ihren 53er zum 63er machen können. Fast.

Meistens sehen 10 Jahre alte Wagen aus wie 10 Jahre alte Wagen.
Nicht so der Volkswagen.
Das liegt einmal ganz einfach an seiner Form. Von innen verbessern wir den VW immer und immer wieder. Seine Form verändern wir nicht.

Wozu auch? Sie ist vernünftig. Praktisch. Gut durchdacht.
Das liegt zum anderen ganz einfach an seiner Qualität.
Und wenn man den Volkswagen liebevoll pflegt, kann es einem so gehen wie Herrn Paul

Rave in Herne, Westfalen. Er schrieb uns: „10 Jahre habe ich in meinem VW hinter mich gebracht. Und 345000 km. Mein Wagen sieht hoch aus wie neu." Ist das ein Einzelfall? Kaum.
Briefe wie diesen bekommen wir jeden Tag.

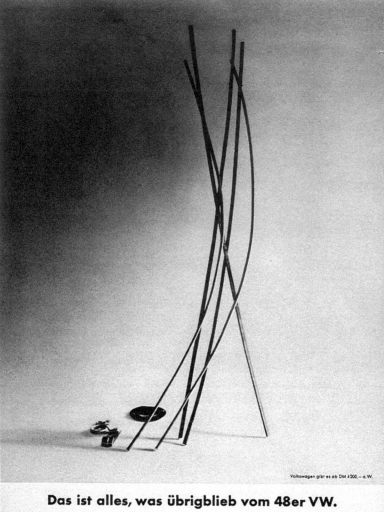

Das ist alles, was übrigblieb vom 48er VW.

7 Teile.
Die. wir in 16 Jahren nicht verbessert haben. (Weil es an ihnen nichts zu verbessern gab.) Deckel für das Abdeckblech vorn. Feder und Bolzen für das Deckelschloß hinten. Führungs-schienen am Abschlußblech vorn und hinten.

Aber den Rest des VW haben wir verbessert.
Von Anfang an. Von hinten bis vorn.
Man sieht diese Verbesserungen nicht auf den ersten Blick. Weil die meisten tief im Innern des VW sind. Aber wenn man seinen VW im dritten, vierten, fünften Jahr fährt, dann merkt man sie.

Daran, daß man nichts merkt. (Weil selten etwas kaputtgeht.) Wer einen vernünftigen Wagen baut und will, daß er vernünftig bleibt, der muß ihn ständig verbessern. Nichts ande-res bleibt ihm übrig.

In 1959 Hahn laid the foundation for the international beetle advertising continuing to be a guideline up to this day. The following pages present some of the most original motifs in the Beetle advertising campaign of the Doyle Dane Bernbach Agency (DDB) and LASTRI (Brazil).

Beetle ads

Niemand ist vollkommen.

In den letzten 18 Jahren haben wir ziemlich gut gelernt, wie man einen guten Wagen baut.

Heute hat dieser Wagen den Ruf, ein vollkommener Wagen zu sein.

Und wir haben 7306 Inspekteure, die aufpassen, daß sein Ruf keine Schramme bekommt.

Diese harten Männer bezahlen wir dafür, daß sie Dinge finden, zu denen sie nein sagen.

Nein heißt Nein.

Sie stoppen jeden VW kleiner Dinge wegen, die Sie wahrscheinlich nie bemerkt hätten.

Ein vergessener Steppstich im Polster. Ein Staubkorn im Lack.

Oder eine Schramme im Chrom.

Nun ist alles für die Katz, wenn Sie sich eines Tages mit einem kaputten Stoßdämpfer auf dem Marktplatz von Syracus, Sizilien, wiederfinden.

Dann brauchen Sie nur in die Via Archis 15/A zu gehen, und nach Carmelo Ortisi zu fragen.

4896 VW-Service-Stationen sorgen dafür, daß Sie sich sogar in den verlassensten Gegenden Europas nie verlassen zu fühlen brauchen. (Und daß Sie einen Stoßdämpfer bekommen, wenn Sie ihn brauchen.)

Bei all dieser Mühe haben wir bis heute niemanden gefunden, der die Nägel findet, bevor sie Ihnen die Luft aus den Reifen lassen.

Niemand ist vollkommen.

Hier sehen Sie den ersten Wagen von Antarctica.

Dies ist der erste VW im Südpolgebiet. Er ist das erste Fahrzeug in der Antarktis, das nicht speziell für die Antarktis gebaut ist.

Wie Raupenschlepper, Traktoren, Hundeschlitten. R. McMahon, Leiter einer australischen Forschungsgruppe, fährt diesen Wagen.

Über Eis. Durch Schnee. Bei 32 Grad unter Null.

Er fährt ihn nicht zum Vergnügen.

Er fährt ihn als Erkundungswagen. Als Begleitfahrzeug für Traktorenzüge. Als Schlepper für Hundeschlitten.

McMahon: „Der Wagen fährt, als sei er speziell für die Antarktis gebaut."

Falls Sie, statt durch die Eiswüste, durch die Wüste fahren wollen:

Wir haben auch einen Wagen, der speziell für die Wüste gebaut zu sein scheint.

Mit Sonnendach.

Er ist klein, hat wenig Chrom und ist importiert.
Was macht ihn dann zum viertgrößten Auto in Amerika?

Zunächst war er drüben mehr ein Ulk. Die Tankwarte suchten vorn nach dem Motor. Auf der Fifth Avenue gab es einigen Auflauf, als dort der erste Käfer parkte. Und gleich an ein paar Dutzend Colleges untersuchten die Studenten, wieviel Leute man in dieses Unikum hineinbekommt. (Weltrekord: 23)

Heute findet ihn kaum einer mehr komisch. Vor allem nicht die Konkurrenz: In der Verkaufsstatistik steht der VW 1300 vor 169 anderen amerikanischen Wagen-

typen an vierter Stelle.

Die Leute hatten sich zunächst wohl weniger für den VW als gegen Detroit entschieden. Sie waren das viele Blech leid.

Später merkten sie, daß das Ding auch fuhr. Ein bißchen schneller sogar als die Polizei auf den Highways erlaubt.

Sie lernten zu schätzen, ohne Mühe in fast jede Parklücke hineinzukommen.

Sie fanden es jetzt selbstverständlich, daß man für eine Beule im Kotflügel nicht

gleich das halbe Auto renovieren muß. Sondern nur den Kotflügel auswechselt. Für ein paar Dollar. (Nicht jeder Amerikaner heißt Rockefeller.)

Sie können kaum noch verstehen, warum ein Auto nach wenigen Jahren klappern muß.

Und daß der Volkswagen importiert ist, haben viele Amerikaner schon fast vergessen. Für sie ist der Käfer amerikanisch geworden. Wie die Frankfurter Würstchen.

VW

VW 6242 B Er ist klein . . .
Spiegel Nr. 17 vom 18. 4. 66
1/1 S., s/w.
4566 PA

Walt Disneys neuer Star kommt aus Wolfsburg.

In den großen amerikanischen Uraufführungskinos läuft und läuft und läuft seit Wochen vor ausverkauften Häusern ein turbulenter Farbfilm der Walt-Disney-Produktion: „The Love Bug". („Ein toller Käfer.")

Die Hauptrolle in diesem abendfüllenden Jux spielt niemand anderes als unser Käfer aus Wolfsburg.

Er heißt Herbie und treibt einundhalb Stunden lang eine Menge Unfug. Er reißt nachts von zu Hause aus, liebt Irish Coffee und gewinnt — auf reichlich unorthodoxe Weise — Wettrennen gegen weit schnellere und teurere Rivalen.

Wir in Wolfsburg sind natürlich mächtig stolz auf Herbie. Zumal die Disney-Leute ohne unser Zutun auf die Idee gekom-

Das ist Herbie aus Walt Disneys neuem Film „Ein toller Käfer".

men sind, einen Film mit dem Käfer zu machen.

Warum eigentlich?

Ganz einfach. Sie versprechen sich von ihrem neuen Star ein Geschäft. Denn der Käfer ist auf der ganzen Welt beliebt. „Wohl kein Auto . . . hat soviel Zuneigung und Zärtlichkeit geweckt wie der Käfer aus Wolfsburg, Germany", schrieb unlängst ein amerikanischer Publizist. Und er hat wohl recht. Denn wie hätten wir sonst 12 Millionen Käfer verkaufen können.

Vielleicht sehen Sie Herbie demnächst auch in Ihrem Theater. Außerdem können Sie den neuen Star nach wie vor bei jedem VW-Händler besichtigen.

Er hat keine Allüren.

Typen wie Herbie gibt es ab DM 4525,– o. W. inkl. Umsatzsteuer.

110

Wie lange werden wir die Linie halten?

Hier ist nicht die Rede von der verrauten Linie.
Sondern von der Idee, die dahintersteckt. Einen praktischen, zuverlässigen, wirtschaftlichen Wagen zu bauen, der auf der ganzen Linie vernünftig ist. Und bleibt.

Diese Idee haben wir verwirklicht. Mit einer ganzen Ideen-Kollektion. Luftgekühlter Heckmotor. Einzeln aufgehängte Räder. Drehstabfederung. Glatte Bodenplatte.
Als unsere eigenen Linienrichter haben wir alles immer wieder überdacht.

Und immer wieder verbessert.
Wir werden wohl nie aufhören, unseren Wagen zu verbessern.
Nur eins werden wir beibehalten.
Die große Linie.

VW ab DM 4200. – a. W.

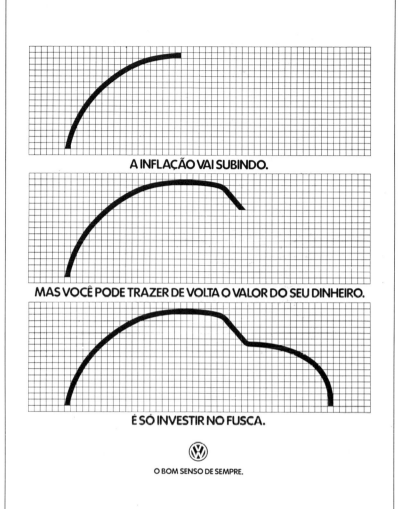

A INFLAÇÃO VAI SUBINDO.

MAS VOCÊ PODE TRAZER DE VOLTA O VALOR DO SEU DINHEIRO.

É SÓ INVESTIR NO FUSCA.

O BOM SENSO DE SEMPRE.

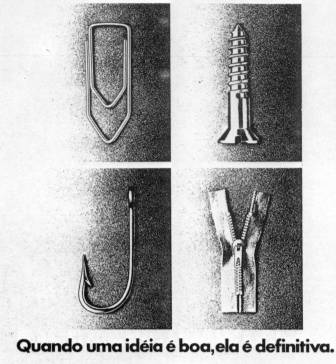

Quando uma idéia é boa, ela é definitiva.

Fusca. Bom hoje, bom amanhã, bom sempre.

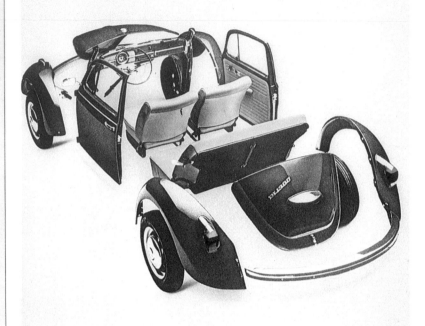

Das haben wir diesmal verbessert.

Alles, was Sie da sehen, haben wir in diesem Herbst am VW 1300 und am VW 1500 verbessert. Und einiges, was Sie nicht sehen können.

Es ist mehr als je zuvor.

Ein gutes Dutzend Verbesserungen ist allein dazu da, den Käfer noch sicherer zu machen.

Zum Beispiel die Zweikreis-Bremsanlage. Die auch dann noch funktioniert, wenn eines der beiden Leitungssysteme ausfallen sollte. (Was Sie wohl kaum erleben werden.)

Und die Sicherheitslenksäule. Das Sicherheitslenkrad. Die neuen Scheinwerfer mit senkrechten Streuscheiben. Die Scheibenwischer mit zwei Geschwindigkeiten. Die Sicherheitsspiegel innen und außen. Die breiteren, stärkeren und höher angebrachten Stoßstangen.

Auch für den Komfort haben wir einiges getan.

Die angenehmste Neuerung ist zweifellos die Frischluftbelüftung. Sie können die Luftzufuhr an zwei Knöpfen getrennt für links und rechts regeln. Und brauchen nicht mehr den lauten und zugigen Fahrtwind durch die Fenster hereinzulassen.

Neu ist auch, daß man jetzt die Beifahrertür auf- und zuschließen kann.

Und daß man zum Tanken nicht mehr die vordere Haube zu öffnen braucht: Der Tankeinfüllstutzen ist jetzt außen rechts hinter einer Federklappe.

Was nicht neu ist, ist der Preis. Die beiden Käfer kosten keinen Pfennig mehr als bisher.

Ist das nicht auch eine hübsche Verbesserung?

2 shapes known the world over.

Nobody notices Coke bottles or Volkswagens any more.

They're so well known, they blend in with the scenery.

It doesn't matter what the scenery is, either. You can walk in and buy a VW in any one of 136 countries.

And that takes lots of scenery.

Deserts. Mountains. Hot places. Cold places. Volkswagens thrive.

Hot and cold don't matter; the VW engine is air-cooled. It doesn't use water, so it can't freeze up or boil over.

And having the engine in the back is what makes all the difference when it comes to mud

and sand and snow.

The weight is over the power wheels and so the traction is terrific.

VWs also get along so well wherever they are because the service is as good in Tasmania as it is in Toledo.

(The only reason you can't buy a VW at the North Pole is that Volkswagen won't sell you one. There's no VW service around the corner.)

We hear that it's possible to buy yourself a Coke at the North Pole, though.

Which makes us suspect there's only one thing that can get through ahead of a Volkswagen.

A Coke truck.

Dealer Name

VW 2579-71

The $35,000 Volkswagen.

Have we gone stark raving mad?

No, but when we heard this car was on display at the Los Angeles International Auto Show, we thought somebody had.

As it turned out, there was a method to the owner's madness.

Why not transform the world's best known economy car into the world's most economical limousine?

After all, a lot of the things that make great luxury cars great are already there in the humble little Bug.

Like 23 years of perfecting every single part of the car.

And subjecting it to over 16,000 different inspections before we sell it to you.

And having it worth lots of money to you when you sell it to someone else.

So why not stretch it out to limo length?

Why not add an intercom, bar and mahogany woodwork and tufted English upholstery and a carriage lamp to signal the doorman?

Why not be the savingest millionaire on the road?

That, children, is exactly how the rich get richer.

VW 2572-71

Presenting the 84 mpg Volkswagen.

Since all the car manufacturers are conducting their own mileage tests these days, we at Volkswagen thought we'd conduct one too.

So we modified our body—and our engine. And, of course, we got someone who didn't weigh much to drive.

Lo and behold, we got 84 miles per gallon! Ridiculous? Nobody normally drives like this? Of course. That's precisely our point. Nobody normally drives like most of those tests you're seeing.

Volkswagen: An honest 25*miles per gallon.

Some shapes are hard to improve on.

Ask any hen.

You just can't design a more functional shape for an egg.

And we figure the same is true of the VW Sedan. Don't think we haven't tried. (As a matter of fact, the Volkswagen's been changed nearly 3,000 times.)

But we can't improve our basic design. Like the egg, it's the right kind of package for what goes inside.

So that's where most of our energy goes. To get more power without using more gas. To put synchromesh on first gear. To improve the heater. That kind of thing

As a result, our package carries four adults, and their luggage, at about 32 miles to a gallon of regular gas and 40,000 miles to a set of tires.

We've made a few external changes, of course. Such as push-button doorknobs.

Which is one up on the egg.

Der VW läuft   und läuft   und läuft   und läuft

und läuft   und läuft   und läuft   und läuft

und läuft   und läuft   und läuft   und läuft

und läuft   und lauft   und läuft   und läuft

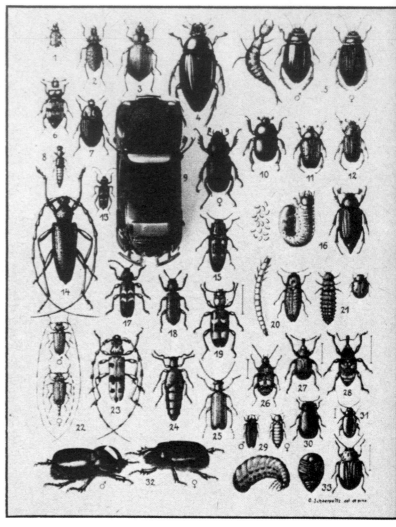

Beetle medley

Fan cult

Views

Dollar Beetle

Customs clearance – according exactly to the rules . . .

"You know, I love to reminisce about our Sunday excursions!"

Invention of ancient Beetle by a clever man of the late Diluvium

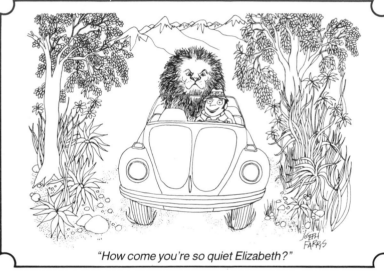

"How come you're so quiet Elizabeth?"

"I asked you to hear the witness and measure the track, not vice-verse!"

Beetle of the month

Beetle of the month
Courtesy GUTE FAHRT Magazine

Washed too hot!

"Deal of the month"

Personnel carrier for the Volkswagen-board members

Nothing is too much for the true Beetle enthusiast! (Courtesy Peter Aschwanken)

The Beetle is held in high esteem as mobile home too, whether with hardtop or with tent extension or converted in Do-it-yourself tradition

Beetle variety

Beetle as "Woodie" by Wendler in Reutlingen

As van with tilt by Drews in Wuppertal

As pick-up by Beutler in Switzerland

As "Variant" by Beutler

And by Meeussen in Antwerp/Belgium

Or as delivery van with shutters (Beutler)

as pick-up

with wooden platform

and load area

"Special Delivery" by B.G.W. Limited (USA)

"Vandetta" by Gundaker (USA)

The US company Fenderprize offers a complete range of other interesting accessories for Beetle beautification, in addition to these fender skirts.

How many horses are lurking under the bonnet here?

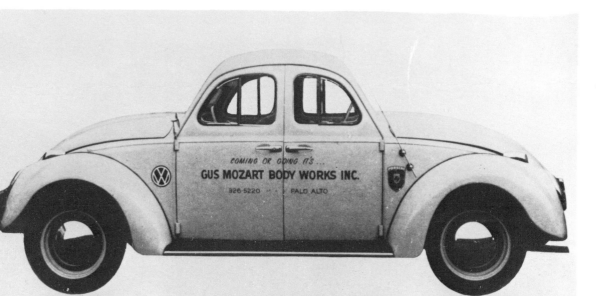

Front or rear?

An extra-long wheelbase Beetle with luxurious interior and four doors was presented in 1969 by the US company Troutman & Barnes. $ 35,000 was the price tag on the Luxury Beetle.

Beetle with modified front section

as Opera coupé

as two-windows cabrio

as Baja-Bug

as Turbo Beetle

"Chopped" version

street-legal or all-terrain

individually styled

126

A Beetle in spite of everything

With four end-pipes and slotted bonnet

With plastic accessories

With porthole

Open engine: Baja Bug

As "Shady Lady"

With "Air brake" spoiler

In Mercedes look

With side pipes

Albar Beetle from Switzerland

Can-Can or Can-Am Beetle?

With eight cylinder Chevrolet powerplant

One-horsepower Beetle without . . .

. . . and with roof

Beetle trailer . . .

. . . as enclosed trike . . .

. . . and topless

Beetle as amphibian: The Australian Paul Greene with his "Sea Bug".

Beetles for any occasion

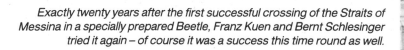

Exactly twenty years after the first successful crossing of the Straits of Messina in a specially prepared Beetle, Franz Kuen and Bernt Schlesinger tried it again – of course it was a success this time round as well.

Even in the Irish Sea the amphibian Beetle is at home, here is Malc Buchanan with his amphibian Volkswagen.

Beercan Regatta in Darwin/Australia. Hundreds of empty beercans, carefully soldered up, provide the necessary buoyancy.

Amphibian Beetle in America

This Beetle went for an unexpected swim in Copenhagen, It fell into the harbour; it took the fire department to haul it back onto dry land.

There are amphibian Beetles in Sweden, too.

Service Beetle on rails in Ontario/Kanada

as roller for smoothing the way and with bumper guards somewhere in Australia

as Coupé de Ville

Chevy Beetle

Beetle as cablecar in Switzerland

. . . Agricultural Beetle: ploughing . . .

. . . overgrown with grass

"Car Stuffing" is the name of this Beetle sport which comes from the USA: As many people as possible must pack into a Beetle in as short a time as possible; car stuffing is already a popular Beetle sport here and particularly in Sweden.

Workshop billboard in the USA and as workshop sign in Germany

Promotion gimmick in a tea house in Tokyo

. . . and on a roof in Hamilton, Canada

△ Reflections

Mobile home ▽

Beetle art on the garage door ▽

Sun, sand and . . . Baja Bug (Copacabana, Rio de Janeiro)

Colourful Beetle parade

snazzily painted

. . . tastefully finished in the Wolfsburger AutoMuseum

... colour printed as flower Beetle

tin box look

... as western Beetle

... and Satans Bug

Schloß Neuschwanstein was fairy godmother to this Beetle

The beauty and the beast: Spick and span as show-tuning Beetle and for 1000 Marks at the Oldtimer flea market

. . . finished à la "Starsky & Hutch"

. . . runs (almost) without petrol

What might be underneath?

CLASSIC BEETLES: Veteran gathering in Bad Camberg

51 export model, the two-tone finish was not standard then, however

Fully restored: 1948 Beetle

Beetle convertible from Karmann with (standard) two-tone finish

The Beetle as filmstar

One-off: ROLO Beetle as advertising gimmick – Beetle from two Beetles

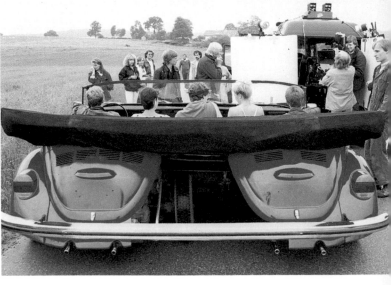

The Beetle is not the only "typically German" product around

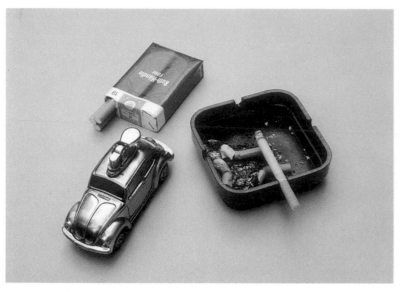

Beetle as cigarette lighter

. . . as sterling silver key-ring

. . . as fine silver plaque

. . . as penknife

... filled with after shave

. . . or whiskey

. . . as collage assembled from clock components

as a bus stop

Ceramic Beetle as table lamp

. . . as small flower vase

. . . as money-box

. . . also exciting as a toy

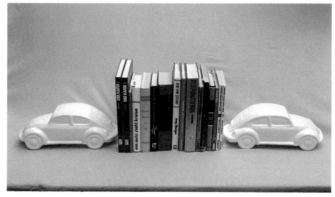

. . . indispensable as bookend, too

Time-honoured: Beetle as grandfather clock

. . . as Stefan's potty and as toilet paper holder

148

Hand-knitted Beetle

... baked

Stefan's cushion

Nichts geht
über die
Verläßlichkeit.

... embroidered

Beate's skirt

Dawn with pullover and knitted cap

Beetles in all variations

Fascination from Singapore: Beetle as transformer

Beetle with jet propulsion

Cross Beetle in 1:10 scale with electric motor and remote control from ROBBE

LEGO Beetle made up of 4700 individual building bricks

. . . as a fifties advertising gift (WIKING)

151

Beetle in kit form

. . . with clockwork

Beetle for Z, N and HO gáuges

. . . as service vehicle

. . . in all sizes

. . . as wooden toy

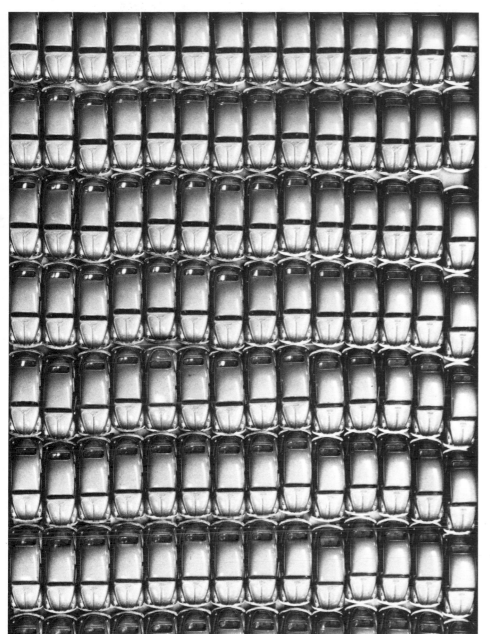

Beetle production in the SIKU factory (Scale 1:55)

Beetle showcase for the Beetle collector

◁ △

Ceramic Beetle as teapot and as showpiece

▽

The only Beetle with front wheel drive

*Beetle as
a sand castle*

as a cake

Volkmar Jungk collects Beetles the way other people collect stamps

Chocolate Beetles

Mini Beetle with lawnmower engine

. . . as lolly

as a candle *as an eggcup* *for important messages*

Beetle as key board

. . . as belt buckle

Beetle as key-ring

Jubilee plaque

Beetle-wrist-watch

Riepenhausen-Stoll Beetle with large luggage compartment

Beetle curious: hand-crafted

Mirror images

as air freight

Snow Beetle

DER LETZTE FÜR DEUTSCHLAND
PRODUZIERTE KÄFER AUS MEXICO
DESDE MEXICO CON AMOR

Puebla/Mexico, July 25, 1985: The last VW Beetles destined for Europe are being shipped to Emden/Germany.

Birthday present from "praliné": a pretzel window beetle at a scale of HO (1:87).

▲ Odd: On the occasion of its 50th birthday the Beetle turned into a Beatle – out of marzipan.

◄

Wolfsburg, October 17, 1985: birthday party with more than 500 congratulants from all over the world.

▼

Limited edition: 2400 anniversary models to celebrate the Beetle's birthday.